CONTENTS

INTRODUCTION

I

In the introduction to his recent volumes upon the Elizabethan Drama,[1] Mr. Schelling outlines the field he covers as follows : —

" We could find no better date than 1600 as a point of departure from which to map out the physical dimensions, so to speak, of our subject. If we mark thirty-seven years backward, we have the date of the birth of Shakespeare, 1564; thirty-seven years forward, and we have the date of the death of Ben Jonson, 1637, Shakespeare's greatest contemporary in his own field. If we add five years, backward and forward, to these two lapses of thirty-seven years, we have the period from the accession of Queen Elizabeth, 1558, to the outbreak of the Civil War in 1642. Indeed, this symmetry of dates — for the statement of which we are indebted to that indefatigable if vexatious scholar, F. G. Fleay, — extends into other points. The career of Shakespeare stretched, roughly speaking, from 1589 to 1611, eleven years on either side of 'the meeting-point of the centuries'; and again, the first Elizabethan structure built expressly for dramatic presentations, and called the Theatre *par excellence*, was erected in 1576, twenty-four years before our point of departure; while the last theatre to be rebuilt, before the advancing tide of Puritanism swept all such landmarks as

[1] *Elizabethan Drama, 1586–1642*, by FELIX E. SCHELLING. Boston: Houghton Mifflin Company, 1908, vol. i, p. xxxv.

this before it, was the Fortune, in 1624, the same dis-
tance of time onward.

" Within these eighty-four years arose and flourished
in the city of London, then of a population not exceeding 125,000 souls, over a score of active and enter-
prising theatrical companies, averaging some four or five
performing contemporaneously, and occupying at different times some twenty theatres and inn yards fitted
up for theatrical purposes. Among these actors were
Edward Alleyn, who made his repute in the title rôles
of *Tamburlaine*, *The Jew of Malta*, and *Doctor Faus-
tus*; Richard Burbage, the original Richard III, and
perhaps the first to play Hamlet, Lear, and Othello;
John Lowin, the creator of the rôles of Jonson's *Sejanus* and *Volpone*, and of Sir Epicure Mammon;
and, of a lesser degree as an actor, though not as a
manager, William Shakespeare. Within these eighty-
four years wrote and starved, or occasionally acquired
competence, a swarm of writers, producing some hun-
dreds of plays, less than half of which are in all proba-
bility now extant. Amongst these authors were a score
of brilliant playwrights, not one of whom but has added
his treasures to that richest of our English inheritances,
the literature of our tongue; and at least six of whom
have written dramas, which, judged as dramas, are beyond the achievements of the greatest of their successors. Within these eighty-four years, in short, arose,
developed, and declined the most universal and imaginative, the most spontaneous and heterogeneous literature in dramatic form which has yet come from the
hand of man."

Compact as this valuable summary is of striking
facts, the attention is arrested, even on a first read-

ing, by the statement that a city with a population of
125,000 gave support so loyal and liberal to the stage
as to render such a drama possible. An absorbed interest on the part of every rank and class of society
was, indeed, a necessary condition of its transcendent
greatness. But one must not make the natural error
of assuming this interest due to the sudden appearance,
in some mysterious way, of men of extraordinary genius, Marlowe, Shakespeare, Ben Jonson, with a score of
others less marvellously gifted — an error found in its
crudest form in the reply returned by undergraduates
to the question why the Elizabethan period was so
great, that " it was great because there were so many
great men then." The Elizabethan period was great
because of the profound change wrought by the Renaissance in the attitude of men towards life; because
England, belated in undergoing its influence, came
suddenly and directly into possession of the results of
this change already attained in other countries, notably
Italy; because a new field of opportunity was opened
for men of ability without respect to social distinction ;
because England was growing in strength and stability
as a national power ; because the Tudors in general —
Elizabeth notably — sincerely cared for, and by their
interest and example fostered, literature; above all,
because the new influences, intense in their quickening
power, wrought in England upon a people which, in
the classes that count most, the yeomanry and peas-
antry, had, for centuries back (however secondary in
inspiration " polite literature " might be), cherished a
deep and abiding love for poetry.

The drama was not the only result, it must be
remembered, of this swift exaltation of the national

genius. But it was its highest expression, and for the
following reasons. The play was already, and had long
been, loved by the people, and had become an organic
part of the national life and a medium for its poetic
expression. The national genius, in fact, characteristically combined, with vigor of imagination and instinct-
ive power of poetic expression, an intense interest in
active and practical life; in diversity of circumstance
as making or marring the fortunes of men; in the play
of human nature in character as affected by or com-
manding circumstance. Moreover, foreign influences
became available to aid and hasten the development of
the popular drama to artistry in conception, content,
and form; and, furthermore, the English genius, while
eager enough to welcome and use these, was too stal-
wart, individual, and independent in its awakened
strength to become subject to them in any servile way,
and adapted or modified them as it pleased, its drama
remaining as it had long been, national and individual,
a drama characteristically English.

The purpose of this volume is to help illustrate
the first of these points — the long development of the
drama that lies behind the great achievements of
the Elizabethans, the native genius inherent in it, the
important part it played in the nation's imaginative
life. To this end it presents certain selected plays to
exemplify the several typical stages of development.
These plays are translated because, simple matter as it
may be to gather the general sense from the original
Middle English, the constant recurrence of obsolete
words and phrases prevents many persons from gaining
a really complete and fully enjoyable understanding of
the dialogue. The volume is primarily intended for

reading in the limited time available in outline courses
in English literature, and as a convenient introduction
to the subject for the student and general reader.[1]
Those who wish to pursue the subject in greater detail
may read the *Medieval Stage* of Mr. E. K. Chambers,
which includes, and, to an impressive degree, enlarges
upon its predecessors in the field, and follow it with Mr.
Schelling's masterly exposition of the development of
the Elizabethan drama, as a result of the varying balance of native conditions and external influences, from
its far origins in this medieval drama.

II

THE RISE OF THE RELIGIOUS PLAY

There is no connection between the classic stage and
the medieval drama. The medieval drama represents a
new beginning. When the dramatic performances, pub-
lic and private, of the later Roman Empire fell justly
under the ban of the Church and disappeared, the place
of the actor was taken by the wandering minstrel, acrobat, juggler, and exhibitor of trained animals, whose
entertainments in hall, " bower," and street formed a
chief source of amusement in medieval life apart from
athletic games and the chase. Among the minstrels, the
dramatic instinct led to impersonations similar in character to those of the elocutionist of our own day, in

---

[1] Those who wish a wider range of plays may refer to Schelling's
Elizabethan Drama (vol. ii, 442). For the general development, see
the plays included in Manly's *Specimens of the Pre-Shaksperean Drama*
and Gayley's *Representative English Comedies*. Also see Gayley's *Plays
of Our Forefathers*.

which monologue and dialogue were rendered dramatically, though by one person, and sometimes even, it
would seem, with use of characteristic costume. Certain religious poems, indeed, designed to be read for in-
struction (the *Cursor Mundi* and the fragment *Judas*
may serve for examples), show plainly that they were
intended to be delivered dramatically.[1]

Also, but in a much more important way, the dramatic instinct found expression in dramatic dances,
games, and folk-plays. These had existed from the
earliest times, some of the dances and games going
back to remote pagan festivities. In these dances and
games, certain prescribed figures and movements were
executed, typifying plainly, in many cases, myths long
forgotten, such as the death of winter and the reawak-
ening of spring. The sword dance, common throughout
England in various forms, in which the dancers carried
swords and slashed at each other, evidently originated
as a mimic representation of war. Familiar examples
are the May-day games, and the Morris dancers with
their characters drawn in part from the story of Robin
Hood. A more developed form of drama, with spoken dialogue and a semblance of plot, is found in the folk-plays,
or mummings. We may feel certain that from the earliest times, though no record remains of them, plays were
naturally improvised, or even planned for special oc-
casions, just as children to-day, who know nothing of
the theatre, improvise in their play what are essentially
little dramas. Of the later folk-plays we have examples
numerous enough. Two are given in this volume, the

---

[1] One early work, the *Harrowing of Hell*, though in dramatic form,
was, it is now generally believed, intended only to be read or "delivered."

Robin Hood Plays, and the mumming of St. George, or *St. George Play*, the latter in a version recorded, in a much degenerated form, in 1853. For such folk-dances and folk-plays have remained to our own time in parts of England. Kenneth Grahame, in his charming *Golden Age*, refers to the mummers (ed. 1899, p. 117) : " Twelfth-night had come and gone, and life next morning seemed a trifle flat and purposeless. But yester-eve and the mummers were here! They had come striding into the old kitchen, powdering the red brick floor with snow from their barbaric bedizenments ; and stamping, and crossing, and declaiming, till all was whirl and riot and shout. Harold was frankly afraid : unabashed, he buried himself in the cook's ample bosom. Edward feigned a manly superiority to illusion, and greeted these awful apparitions familiarly, as Dick and Harry and Joe. As for me, I was too big to run, too rapt to resist the magic and surprise. Whence came these outlanders, breaking in on us with song and ordered masque and a terrible clashing of wooden swords ? And after these, what strange visitants might we not look for any quiet nights, when the chestnuts popped in the ashes, and the old ghost stories drew the awe-stricken circle close ? . . . This morning, house-bound by the relentless, indefatigable snow, I was feeling the reaction. Edward, on the contrary, being violently stage-struck on this his first introduction to the real Drama, was striding up and down the floor, proclaiming ' Here be I, King Gearge the Third,' in a strong Berkshire accent."

The folk-play, as developed from and as fostering a native dramatic instinct, is of the greatest possible importance, but it also had a direct and most important influence in shaping the formal drama, as we shall see later in the proper place. To the development of the formal drama we now pass.

III

THE LITURGICAL PLAY

If we may take a wide-spread natural impulse towards dramatic expression for granted, how did it take shape in a formal drama with possibilities of a continuous and orderly development?

The answer is that the drama in its organic historical development originated in the Church, which, though it had sternly repressed the classic drama, in time came itself to use dramatic action to enrich its liturgy and to enforce its teachings. The liturgy indeed was in many parts essentially dramatic in conception, the Mass itself, for example. A specific dramatic development began, however, in the elaboration of the liturgy, during the ninth century, by the use of so-called "tropes," or texts appropriate for special days, adapted for choral rendering in the musical portions of the Mass. Some of these tropes were simply lyric, or hymnal, in character; some, involving dialogue, were from the first dramatic in character. Certain tropes used at Easter, Christmas, and Ascension, are of special importance as starting points of dramatic expansion.

None is of greater importance than the *Quem Quæritis* of Easter Day. This trope was based upon the account in the Gospel of the question, " Whom seek ye ? " addressed to the Marys, as they went to

anoint the body of Christ, by the angel who sat beside
the sepulchre, and his announcement to them of the
resurrection. It was originally sung as a choral addition to the music of the Introit of the Mass, that is,
the procession with which the Mass begins. In course
of time, however, as its dramatic possibilities were developed it was detached from this position, where
elaboration in the way of action was impossible, and
inserted in the services preceding the Mass. Usage no
doubt differed in various places, but the famous passage in the *Concordia Regularis*, translated in this
volume, makes it clear that the change had taken place
in England before the end of the tenth century ; it had
taken place probably in France and Germany at an
even earlier date. The passage referred to describes
the ritual in detail as prescribed for use at Winchester
in the tenth century ; in this case the trope, which
had become a brief, but none the less complete, liturgical drama, formed part of the Third Nocturne during Matins on Easter morning.

In the course of time, with great diversity of development in different places, the original *Quem
Quæritis* was enlarged by the addition of dialogue and
of dramatic action, in particular by transferring to it
liturgical plays belonging to other times in the Easter
season, producing a play with several separate scenes.
The original *Quem Quæritis* included a scene between
the angel and the Marys at the sepulchre followed by
a responsive chant between the Marys and the choir
(compare the version of the play used at Winchester,
translated in this volume). In one of the fullest versions which developed from the original form, the
manuscript of which is at Tours, Pilate sets a watch

before the sepulchre, an angel sends lightning and the soldiers fall as if dead, the Marys appear and sing *planctus* or songs of lamentation, there is a scene with a spice-merchant from whom they buy spices to anoint the Saviour's body (the spice-merchant was developed into an important humorous element in later forms of the play in Germany), more *planctus* follow, then comes the *Quem Quæritis* proper, after which follows the announcement of the resurrection to Pilate, the apparition of the risen Christ to Mary Magdalen and the announcement of the resurrection by the Marys to the disciples, the appearance of Christ to the disciples and to Thomas, then a trope (which it is needless to consider here) termed the *Victimæ Paschali*, and at the end the *Te Deum*.

The properties used were at the first very simple. For the sepulchre a symbolic representation made by heaping together the service-books on the altar, or a recessed tomb, if there happened to be one in the chancel, at first sufficed. Later, a special sepulchre, more or less realistic, was often constructed; such sepulchres not uncommonly formed permanent features in medieval churches. A swathed crucifix, representing the dead Christ, was deposited with suitable ceremonies in the sepulchre, and at the proper moment was removed, the cloths which swathed it being left for use in the play. It will be noted that the Winchester ritual prescribes that the cleric who represents the angel shall carry a palm. Such simple symbolism was all that was necessary, but presumably in course of time special costumes and other realistic details were added.

The Christmas liturgical play, representing the visit of the Shepherds to the infant Christ, had a similar history. Just as the Easter play centred about the sepulchre, the Christmas play centred about the *præsepe* or manger, in which the Christ was laid, which was at first depicted symbolically and later realistically, much as it often is now in Catholic churches with Joseph and Mary, and the ox and the ass. Moreover, a trope, modeled directly upon the Easter *Quem Quæritis*, beginning *Quem quæritis in præsepe?* — originally used in the Introit of the third or great Mass, and afterwards transferred to Matins, — seems to have been its starting point. This play, the *Officium Pastorum*, or *Pastores*, and a play taken probably from Holy Innocents' Day, the *Rachel*, the subject of which was the lamentation of Rachel for her children, were in some cases taken up into an Epiphany Play, called the *Tres Reges*, *Magi*, *Herodes*, or *Stella*, representing the visit of the Magi to the Saviour, which centred about a star hung from the nave and lighted by candles. Thus, in more or less elaborate forms in various places, a Christmas cycle developed. One Christmas play, of special importance, the *Prophetæ*, calls for mention. This did not take its rise in a trope, but in a sermon, the *Sermo contra Iudæos, Paganos, et Arianos, de Symbolo*, ascribed erroneously to St. Augustine, which was commonly used as a *lectio*, or lesson, in the Christmas season. The passage in this sermon converted into a play was one in which the homilist calls first upon the Jews to bear witness to Christ, citing for this purpose the prophets, and then calls upon the Gentiles to bear similar witness, citing Virgil (*Eclogues*, iv, 7), Nebuchadnezzar, and the Erythræan Sibyl. This passage was changed into a dialogue with the several prophets speaking in person, clad in appropriate dress and with appropriate symbols. This play of the *Prophetæ* remained as an important part of the great cycles of religious plays to be spoken of later.

We need not touch on the Ascension trope, also modeled on the *Quem Quæritis*. The Christmas, Easter, and Ascension plays were the models for a large number of liturgical plays, and plays of similar general character, which were acted in the church at appropriate seasons, and which became in course of time more and more elaborate and more freely dramatic in character. One of them, a German version of the *Antichrist*, apparently for Advent, was a most elaborate spectacle, requiring a large number of actors, a special stage with representations of a temple of God and seven thrones, and abundant space for marching and countermarching. In this play, it is interesting to note, allegorical figures appear of the Synagogue, Holy Church, Pity, and Justice — a most striking anticipation of the later morality. The addition of new scenes to plays, the addition of new plays for special days, the transfer of plays from lesser feast-days to the great feast-days of their season, went on, but the material extant does not permit the progress of these changes to be traced in detail. Two changes are, however, of such fundamental importance as to demand treatment in a separate section.

IV

THE MIRACLE OUTSIDE THE CHURCH

In course of time — when, it is not possible to say — the presentation of liturgical plays thus elaborated was transferred from within the church to the church-yard, the street or market-place, or to convenient spots in the fields. The cause of this change was not, as often supposed, so much the fact that the plays began to include non-religious elements of a character indecorous for presentation within the church. The real reason was the necessity for more room both for the representation and for the audience.

Furthermore, the control of their presentation passed over to the municipal authorities, into the hands of lay fraternities, or, generally and characteristically, into the hands of the town gilds, that is, the associations of men pursuing the same crafts, such as the butchers, tanners, tailors, weavers, and the like. As the plays became elaborated, the increased number of actors and cost of production made it difficult for the plays to be given with the help only of the lower clergy and scholars from the church schools, and without some division of the labor and cost. When we are first able to find somewhat complete information concerning the religious play, we find it carefully organized by the civic authorities, the different plays or scenes being assigned to the various gilds, each gild being responsible for the proper production of its play and for its share of the general expense.

Important results directly followed. The language of the country took the place of Latin in the dialogues, either in part, or, in most cases, wholly. The acting became more dramatic, scenes that permitted it were made more realistic, and scenes were invented that were not in the Bible story. Certain of the characters took on a new dramatic life and interest quite separate from their part in the Bible story. Herod and Pilate, at first given swelling speeches to indicate their importance, became typical braggarts. Herod, notably, became the type of a bullying tyrant ; Shakespeare's phrase " out-Herod Herod " will be remembered. Noah's wife became a shrew and scold ; she refuses to go into the ark, a picture of obstinacy, till the rain drives her in. The life of Mary Magdalen before her conversion is used to present pictures of profligate luxury. The racial and local character of the people acting the plays became impressed upon them. In brief, the miracle plays, originally in a general way alike in all countries or parts of a country, owing to their transfer without the church and out of ecclesiastical control, became secularized, nationalized, and localized, and their dramatic quality intensified.

A result of very great importance, due to their being played out of doors, was the tendency, owing to the inclemency of the winter and spring weather, to shift their production from their proper season to a time when they could be performed and seen with greater enjoyment. A favorite day was Whitsuntide, but much more frequently the chosen day was the high feast of Corpus Christi, finally instituted after an intermission of its earlier observance in 1311, which was celebrated the Thursday after Trinity Sunday. This feast commemorated a miracle which was believed to have given ocular evidence of transubstantiation, that is, the change of the bread and wine of the sacrament to the actual Body and Blood of Christ, and its characteristic feature was, and in certain Continental cities is still, a procession in which the Host was carried through the streets so as to make a circuit of the parish or town. The performance of the plays became associated with the procession, and originally formed part of it. The plays

were given on platforms provided with wheels, called
" pageants," which had two floors, the lower, shrouded
with curtains, supplying dressing-room and retiring-
place, and the upper, covered with a canopy and open
on every side, forming the stage. The pageants were
sometimes adapted to the requirements of the particular play performed on them. For example, on pageants
for certain plays, hell was represented below the stage
as a huge head with gaping mouth belching flame, and,
for the play of Noah, the pageant was shaped like an
ark. These pageants probably formed part, originally,
of the procession itself on Corpus Christi Day, and the
plays were given in succession at the several stations
or halting places where special ceremonies were performed in connection with the Host. Later, when the
popularity of the plays interfered with the real purpose
of the procession, they were separated from it, but the
convenient method of presenting the plays on the pageants which could be moved from place to place in the
town, enabling many persons to see the plays conven-
iently, was retained. It is interesting to note that in
one case at least the plays were given on the feast-day
itself, and the procession was put off to the day after.

The change of the plays of various seasons to a single
day led to the formation of great "cycles," or series,
of plays, in which the original plays came to be something like scenes in a long continued play — there are
forty-eight plays in one cycle, the York plays — representing the great events recorded or prophesied in the
Bible from the Fall of the Angels, or from Creation, to
the Day of Judgment. New plays were added to fill
in gaps, and the plays were subjected to more or less
constant revision and improvement. Beside these great

groups, there were independent Bible plays, and plays on saints' lives, but these are of minor importance beside the great cycles. We have seen that the liturgical play existed in England in Anglo-Saxon times, but it is possible, even probable, that the miracle-play in its developed form was introduced by the Normans. There is record of Bible and saints' plays in the twelfth century in England, but the systematic presentation of Bible plays is usually assumed to date about 1250. They became a vital part of English life, and remained so from the reign of Henry II to Elizabeth's reign, reaching the height of their popularity during the fourteenth and fifteenth centuries.

The historical name in England for all religious plays is *miracle*, a term applied in France, where it originated, to saints' plays only. In France a play on a Bible subject was called a *mystère*, or " mystery ; " this term, generally employed in scholarly literature on the subject till recently, is exotic in English use, and was first employed in the eighteenth century. It has now been discarded for the original inclusive English term *miracle*.

Of the many miracles which once existed, there remain a few independent plays and fragments of cycles, and beside these, most fortunately, four complete cycles, three belonging to the towns of York, Chester, and Wakefield (usually called the " Towneley cycle " from the family that owned the manuscript), and the so-called *Ludus Coventriæ* (also called " Hegge" plays), which did not probably, despite their name, belong to Coventry, where a quite different cycle, now lost, is known to have been given. Though relatively few miracle plays have survived, there still remain over one hundred and fifty different scenes treated in a still larger number of plays.

The pageants, or movable stages, have been described. In some cases, plays were given instead on fixed booths in the market-place or fields, the several booths representing different places; and as the scenes changed, the actors went from one to another by passing through the group of spectators. Parts of the plays were commonly acted on the ground before the pageants or the fixed stages; it was a regular feature for the devils issuing from hell to seize upon and torment spectators to the intense delight of other onlookers. The staging was usually arranged to represent several different scenes at once; thus in the *Second Shepherds' Play* given in this volume, the moor might occupy one side, Mak's house the other, with the stable for the Nativity, covered with a curtain till the proper time, in the middle. The actors were, it seems plain, members of the gilds to which the production of the plays was intrusted, though minstrels and musicians seem to have been called in at times to furnish music. The actors were paid; the performer of the part of God at Coventry (Chambers, vol. ii, 139) received 3s. 4d., the man who hanged Judas 4d., and 4d. more for cock-crowing, a soul, saved or damned, received 20 m., and a " word of conscience " 8d. The properties and costumes were of the simplest; some of the records which remain concerning them are quaint and amusing. The Norwich grocers (Chambers, vol. ii, 141) possessed for a play of Adam and Eve, in addition to the pageant and its fittings, " coats and hosen " for the characters, the serpent's being fitted with a tail, a "face" and hair for God the Father, hair for Adam and Eve, and a " rib colored red." In the

Coventry *Doomsday*, the hell was provided with fire, a windlass, and a barrel for the earthquake. The horses of the Magi at Canterbury were made of hoops, laths and painted canvas. Simple as the properties and dresses were, the gross expense in money, time, and work must have been heavy. The interest and excitement attending a production was very great. The coming performance was ceremoniously announced in advance. The procession of pageants moving slowly from station to station — there were from twelve to sixteen at York — with their many scenes and repetitions was, as Chambers notes, a very lengthy affair. At Chester, three days were necessary. At York, the performance finished in one day, but it started at half past four in the morning.

Two examples of the miracle are included in this volume. One is the Brome *Abraham and Isaac*, selected for its dramatic interest and to serve as a representative of plays from the Old Testament. The other is the *Second Shepherds' Play*, selected to illustrate at once the New Testament plays, and the introduction of additions to the Bible story in its famous " interlude " of Mak, the sheep stealer.

V

THE MORALITY

Liturgical plays continued to exist beside the miracles given in the church, the churchyard, and the streets, which came from them. So also, beside these, developed another, most important type of play, the " morality."

A morality is a moral allegory in the form of a play,

or, as one might better say, a play the subject of which
is a moral allegory. An allegory is a figurative description or narration, that is, the real elements of the description or story are represented under the form of
something else in order to give them greater force and
interest. Thus, for example, in the death of *Blanche
the Duchess*, Chaucer, in place of having the knight
in black who represents John of Gaunt say, "I had
the misfortune to lose my wife," represents him as saying that, while playing at chess with Fortune, Fortune
took his queen. So, similarly, Bunyan represents the
life of a good man, beset by troubles and temptations, as
the pilgrimage of "Christian" to the Heavenly City,
and typifies the experiences which a man meets with
in life in various forms such as "Vanity Fair," the
fight with Apollyon, and Doubting Castle. Personifica-
tion, or the figure of treating inanimate things or abstractions as if they were persons, is always necessary
to allegory, and such personifications serve therefore
in the morality as the characters who, through their
dialogues and action, exemplify the moral truth which
happens to be the subject of the plot or story. These
characters are abstractions of any necessary kind —
Vice, Virtue, or any particular vice or virtue, Mankind, the Seven Deadly Sins (in one character or
separately), the Christian Virtues, Pride of Life, the
World, the Flesh, Learning, Experience, Mind, Will,
Understanding, Youth, Age, Holy Church, Riches,—
in short any social institution, relation, or distinction.
In presenting the moral story, these abstractions talk
and act like real persons, and by their talk and action
make clear and enforce the moral truth which is its
subject.

The cause of development of this type of play can be readily explained. The miracle plays, besides teaching the facts of the Bible stories they portrayed, enforced moral truths as well. In other forms of literature, religious and didactic literature in earlier times, and later in secular literature, allegory had been used for centuries. Nothing could be more simple than the transition from the use of personified abstractions as characters in allegorical narrative to the use of such characters in a play. The development does not seem to have been a gradual one, brought about by the addition to miracle plays of personified abstractions used as characters. This might have been possible in plays on certain subjects, such as Antichrist, for example, or the life of Mary Magdalen before her conversion, with no well-defined Bible story to be followed, but the transition, so far as there was one, was not of this kind. The morality seems to have resulted from the wish to present themes which, because of their nature, did not provide a story and characters, as the Bible stories did; since a story and characters had, accordingly, to be provided, recourse was had naturally to the familiar mode of the allegory. This is best exemplified in the earliest morality recorded, a dramatization of the Paternoster, or Lord's Prayer, dating 1378. The Lord's Prayer was believed in its several petitions to afford aid against the assaults of the seven deadly sins, and the drama made from it took the form of a contest for the soul of man between these sins and the corresponding Christian virtues. The further development of the type is easily understood when the common use of allegory elsewhere, the extended opportunity for original dramatic invention it afforded, and the habit of the medieval mind to personify vices and virtues as conscious agents, of similar kind to angels and devils, are considered. It is worth noting that, in a recent article in *Modern Philology*, Mr. Manly, because of the scarcity of plays intermediate in type between the miracle and the morality, and the apparent suddenness of the appearance of the morality, has likened this seemingly sudden development of a new species to the direct production of new and permanent varieties of plants *per saltum* (in place of through the long gradual development predicated by Darwinian theory), proof of which has recently been given by the experiments of DeVries upon the evening primrose. The analogy is striking because of its interest and suggestiveness, even though not justified by logical similarity of the things, conditions, and processes involved.

The morality is of special interest because it gave additional opportunity for invention, and thereby effected a significant advance towards the secular drama. The extant moralities display confusedly but unmistakably this advance. In them, a definitely religious intention can be seen grading into religious controversy, then into a didactic purpose other than religious (for example, enforcement of the value of learning), and finally into something approaching realistic satire of contemporaneous life. Earlier moralities are typically cyclic; they attempt to picture the life of man from birth to death as subject to the conflict between good and evil; for example, in the *Castle of Perseverance*, Mankind (Humanum Genus) holds his castle, with the help of the Virtues, against the Seven Deadly Sins, till finally betrayed by the temptation of Covetousness in his old age, and saved only by the intervention of Bonus An-

gelus, his "good angel." In later moralities, with limitation of subject to a narrower scope, there is a corresponding gain in dramatic quality.

There is no finer example of the simplicity and
appropriateness of these, the serious dignity and ef-
fectiveness of didactic purpose, the dramatic appeal
through graphic characterization, the intensely vital
humor and pathos, which the morality at its best could
attain, than *Everyman*, which in this volume serves as
an example of this type of play. As regards its inclusion in a volume of English plays, it matters little
whether it is itself the original of, or an adaptation
from, the Dutch play of *Elckerlijk*, or whether both
go back to a common source; it became, in any case,
thoroughly English, if not English in origin. The
power of this play is apparent in the reading, but one
who has read it only and has not seen it acted might
perhaps question whether it could carry, save to the
medieval mind, its double appeal as a play and as an
allegory. Those, however, who have seen its recent
representations, will bear witness that in no way does
one stand in the way of the other. The absorbing
dramatic interest and the allegorical significance of the
dialogue and action are absolutely at one, and are followed concurrently as one. One may even go so far as
to say that its moral effect upon the spectator of this
present day is not materially less than that it exercised
in the past, so truly is it a work of genius in its
kind.

VI

THE INTERLUDE

We come next not so much to a new type of play as to the use of a term which marks an important stage in the advance toward the secular play, indeed the attainment of a secular drama. The definition hitherto commonly accepted of the term "interlude" has been a play inserted between parts of another play (that is, a miracle or morality) in order to relieve its seriousness by humor. The more recent view is that the evidence hardly warrants certainty on this point, and that the term may merely mean a play, or dialogue, between two or more persons. The term, as Mr. Chambers makes clear in his discussion of the subject, is not specific in its application. The probable development of its use would seem to be as follows.

We have been concerned with the religious play and the morality in their continuous and organic development. Here we must turn to a use of dramatic or quasi-dramatic forms apart from this. The games and folk-plays have already been spoken of. Apart from these there were municipal pageants, puppet shows, dumb shows or pantomimes, and other forms of dramatic entertainment. As may be supposed, the play as a means of diversion was not confined to the church and the streets. It was also used, along with the arts of the minstrel, the acrobat, the conjuror, and the exhibitor of trained animals, for entertainment in the halls of the nobles and gentry, town corporations, and merchant gilds. Plays thus used are called "plays" or " disguisings " (as being acted in costume), but they are also called interludes. These plays might be specially devised ; they might be akin to the mummings or folk-plays ; or they might be miracles or moralities. Owing to this fact, the term came into general, though not specific, use. But, though general, it possesses a special significance to the student of the drama. How-ever wide its inclusion, because of its original applica-tion to " plays " and " disguisings," it continued to imply a play designed to afford entertainment, whether or no it was designed quite as much to afford edifica-tion. While therefore it does not mean a new type of play, it means something just as important, namely, a change of view on the part of the playwright in respect to the character and purpose of the play. It matters not at all whether the term is used for what is nothing more nor less than a miracle or morality, or for episodes wholly without religious or moral inten-tion acted by themselves or inserted in miracles or moralities. What it implies is that the playwright is consciously using a freer dramatic form, is less sub-ject to the limitations of the didactic intention, is in-venting more freely, feels himself free to admit new and most important dramatic material which had re-mained hitherto foreign to the religious and didactic drama. No better formulation could be given of the notable part played by the interlude in the develop-ment of the secular drama than that of Mr. Schelling (*Elizabethan Drama*, vol. i, 78), "The line between the morality and the interlude, as between the later in-terlude and regular comedy, is artificial at best. But it is clear that the vital principle of the morality was its interest in life and conduct as affecting the actions of men. The vital principle of the interlude was also its interest in life ; but the ulterior end and purpose, guidance to moral action, had been lost and the artistic sense set free. The interlude deals with comedy; it loves what is near and familiar, and its methods are realistic."

So far then as the term "interlude" becomes specific at all, it means a play in which the author may be using old materials or old methods, but in which he is dealing with them freely. This is true even though the playwright be a controversialist like Bishop Bale. An important result of this freedom appears most clearly in John Heywood (born about 1497, died before 1587). Heywood achieved perfect independence, and, as Mr. Schelling has pointed out, to him was owed a clear recognition of the fact that the giving of pleasure was not merely one of the essentials of the drama (this had been tacitly recognized in the early miracle), but the only essential. Thereupon, through recognition of this fact, the artistic principle was set free, and the beginning of artistic development made possible.

The example of the interlude selected for this volume is the earliest example in English. It is the farcical episode of Mak, the sheep-stealer, made a part of the second of the two Shepherds' Plays (originally Nativity plays, belonging to Christmas), of the *Wakefield* or *Townely Cycle.* Here, by way of caution, it must be pointed out that, though this episode is really without any real connection with the Nativity portion of the play, it is not to be called an interlude because it is an episode thrust into a Nativity play ; as Mr. Chambers truly says, the play is a single fabric. It is an interlude because the author, writing a Nativity play, feels himself free to make this piece of realistic low comedy

part of such a play. The work is justly famous. It was
evidently written by a man of original dramatic genius
(he has been called the " Playwright of Wakefield "),
whose hand may be recognized elsewhere in the cycle,
at once by his superior dramatic gifts and by his characteristic use of the difficult tail-rime stanza in which
Mak is written. The reader will not need to have
pointed out to him the delightful realism of the setting
and characterization, the liveliness and humor of the
dialogue, the spirited handling of the action. Conscious
craftsmanship also is evidenced in the opportunities
given the players for by-play, and in the care with
which important points are prepared for earlier in the
dialogue, — for example, Mak's reference to his wife and
numerous children in connection with the plausibility
of the trick used to hoodwink the shepherds. Very
striking also is the sudden change from boisterous fun
to the exquisite tenderness and beauty of the Nativity
scene at the close. The play within recent years (1908)
has been given at four colleges with success. In such
presentations, the Nativity scene may be essayed without apprehension. The picture of the Virgin Mother
bending over the manger where the Child lies between
the ox and the ass, the adoration of the shepherds, the
gifts they offer, cannot fail in their ingenuous and infinitely touching appeal.

VII

HUMOR AND HISTORY

If in the interlude a form of play had developed in
which the dramatist might freely exercise his powers,

by what means did it become wholly secular, entirely
free of the original didactic intention? This it did
through the ever increasing importance of two elements
in the subjects it used — the element of realism and
humor on the one hand, and of history on the other.

The miracle on the Continent made occasional use
of secular subjects from the romance; but this was
wholly occasional and accidental there and without real
significance, and no similar examples exist among the
plays extant in English. But within the miracle play
from an early period the possibility of the secular
drama lay implicit. As noted above, the miracles became in time realistic and humorous. The Biblical
characters became realistic types, and themes, serious
or even tragic, that of Abraham and Isaac for example
(compare the version in this volume), were interpreted
realistically with passages of pathos and humor woven
into the Biblical story by the playwright. With the
morality, a freer choice of subject became possible and
still greater freedom in treatment. The morality ad-
vanced naturally from purely moral teaching to use as
a weapon of controversy and as a means of satirizing
contemporary social and political conditions. Realism
and humor must also have developed into important
elements in the games, folk-plays, the disguisings, and
other entertainments for the hall. The spirit of farcical
humor appeared notably, for example, in the indecorous pranks attending the Feast of Fools and the in-
stallation of Boy Bishops conducted by the minor
ecclesiastics in cathedral churches, which parodied
ecclesiastical ceremonies, and in the revels under the
leadership of the Lord of Misrule at Christmas. In
brief, as the use of plays for purposes of entertainment

rather than for edification increases, the importance of
the element of humor proportionately increases. One
important source of plays purely secular was, therefore, the realistic treatment of personages and situation
in the miracle, satire of contemporary conditions in the
morality, realism and humor in the folk-plays, dumb-
shows, disguisings, and pageants, whose influence
blended with that of the miracle and morality in the
interlude; then the humorous interlude led directly to
the production of farces, whether of character or situation, and ultimately to the various forms of comedy.

The vitalizing element of humor was present in
every form of drama, but, in the religious and moral
drama, there was one element which was rare, indeed
practically absent, namely, the patriotic or historical
element. This might easily have made its appearance
there in the saints' plays — there were, for example,
plays on St. George, now lost; but, in the first place,
plays on the lives of saints do not seem to have been
numerous in England, as on the Continent, and, in the
second place, such plays were more likely to be on
special patron saints than on specifically English saints,
selected because of patriotic feeling. The great col-
lections of the lives of saints called the *Legendaries*
show a certain amount of patriotic feeling as regards
the inclusion of English saints, but to no notable
degree. This was not because the domination of the
Church in matters churchly or religious precluded
patriotic feeling but because in England there was
not, in anything like the same degree, the veneration
of local or national saints which formed an essentially
pagan cult of *loci genii* on the Continent. Furthermore,
the lives of local saints were nothing like so full of

interesting and moving incidents as those of many in the great range of foreign saints. And even though the patriotic element had entered into saints' plays, and they had existed in some quantity, it might not there have become a significant factor, through being over-powered by the religious and didactic purpose. But the patriotic element was a significant factor in the folk-plays, puppet-shows, municipal pageants, and other similar entertainments. These turned naturally for their themes to the past of England, heroes and events historical and legendary, the heroes of ballads and English princes, nobles, outlaws, rebels, and other popular historical characters. As the interlude merged into "regular" drama, these themes were taken up into it, and led to the development of the historical drama as a distinct species. The earlier type of historical plays are merely moralities with historical characters introduced into them with didactic rather than patri-otic intention. But, with the writing of the tragedies under the influence of the tragedies of Seneca (ex-plained below), patriotic spirit evidenced itself in a number of plays on subjects connected with English history and myth, for example, *Gorboduc* (1562), the Latin tragedy *Richardus Tertius* (1579), *Locrine* (1586), *The Misfortunes of Arthur* (1587). At this date, approximately, the more characteristically Eng-lish historical play, or "chronical history," as it is called, begins. Its inspiration was drawn from Eng-land's mounting pride and exultation in the stirring part she was playing in the world' history, and its source was in the more recent of , ฺ long line of chronicles stretching back into the M ฺdle Ages. The importance of these plays is very great. Mr. Schelling

notes (vol. i, 251) that, within the Elizabethan period,
there is record of upwards of two hundred and twenty
titles of plays on themes from English history, biography,
and legend, and that from 1588 to a year or two after
the close of Elizabeth's reign, they must have consti-
tuted more than a fifth of all contemporary plays. In
this connection, it is worth remembering also that
thirteen of Shakespeare's plays are based on subjects
drawn from what was then accepted as the history of
Britain. Moreover, the "chronicle history" was one
of the direct sources of our greatest tragedies, such as
Lear and Macbeth.

In this volume the folk-plays on English themes are
exemplified by the fragments of the *Robin Hood Play*,
which are nothing more nor less than ballads in dramatic form, and the *St. George Play*, already referred
to above. The chronicle histories, even those so early
as *Jack Straw* and the *Famous Victories of Henry V.*,
with the still earlier Senecan plays, are beyond its
scope.

VIII

AMATEUR AND PROFESSIONAL

We have learned to recognize in the term interlude
its loose generic application to freer forms of the older
types of plays, and plays of mixed character derived
from the interaction of the miracle, morality, folk-play,
and disguising, and we have glanced somewhat far
afield to note how the elements of humor and patriotic
spirit aided in the emergence from these of the " regular " drama. We must next inquire how the acting of

plays passed from amateur or quasi-amateur actors to
professional actors. On this point, Mr. Chambers
(vol. ii, 179–198) has, as elsewhere, added materially
to our detailed knowledge of English conditions.

In France, the acting of plays was so entirely in the
control of amateur associations, religious, literary, or
devoted simply to frivolity, that though professional
actors appear early, they do not displace the amateurs
till the close of the sixteenth century. In England, or-
ganizations of this character were few, and of little importance in the general development. In England, the
first point to be noted is that local players of miracles
often presented their plays away from home. So great
was the interest in dramatic productions that the minstrels found their profession interfered with, and in self-
defense turned themselves to the presentation of plays.
There is clear evidence of bodies of professional players, apparently derived from this source, in the latter
half of the fifteenth century. These acted under the
patronage of important persons, just as, at a later date,
we find the various companies in London known by
the names of noble patrons. We next find companies
of players attached to the court from the time of
Henry VII on. These companies traveled at times,
and independent companies, organized for going from
place to place, multiplied in number. They presented
their interludes in the halls, monasteries, gild-cham-
bers, on the village greens, or even in churches. In
certain places there were special rooms or buildings
commonly used for the giving of plays. Of especial importance is the acting of plays in the inn-yard, which
in its typical form with the stable and its loft at the
end and the two buildings with their long galleries

leading to guest-rooms on either side, provided the model for the earlier London theatres.

These professional players did not by any means bring to an end quickly the acting of plays by amateurs. The great cycles acted by the trade-gilds were not affected by them. The occasional acting of special plays by local talent still went on, and was even stimulated by the professional performers of interludes. The schools and universities were active in giving dramatic performances of various kinds; the special direction of this activity is referred to below. At the court in the sixteenth century, performances were regularly given by the gentlemen and the children of the Chapel Royal. Plays, professional or amateur, ultimately distinctively amateur, were given by the Inns of Court, and, though the acting of interludes, except at Christmas, was interdicted by an order of the bench in 1550, notable entertainments by these legal societies at this season continued into the seventeenth century. Later amateur performances were largely confined to the masque, a form of musical and spectacular play, which originated in and centred about the performance of set dances by maskers. These began towards the end of Elizabeth's reign, and reached their greatest vogue, often involving an incredible expenditure of money and the exercise of the utmost skill of the poet, musician, artist, and stage-carpenter, in the reigns of James and Charles.

Mr. Chambers' conclusion is that throughout nearly the whole of the sixteenth century, it remained doubtful whether the future of the drama was to rest in professional or amateur hands. But, none the less, a popular stage, with professional players, had early established itself, its continued existence was never in doubt, and it is difficult to see how the outcome could have been other than it was, sooner or later. The matter does not rest simply in the fact that the use of choir-boys for the acting of plays (for example, the children of the Chapel Royal and of St. Paul's) led to their professional training and the development of the choir-master into a professional stage-manager. These were professionals, but professionals serving in the interest of what may be termed the literary drama, of the court, school, or university. Of greater importance is the question of the vitality of the essentially professional popular drama, as distinguished from this literary drama. The development here becomes plain if the results of professional presentation upon the plays themselves is considered, and the inevitable triumph of the popular professional company. The presentation of interludes by these companies led to the intensification of their dramatic quality. They were cut down, the action made more direct, the characterization sharpened, the humor and pathos strengthened. The didactic intension slackened, and themes of greater popular interest, and of better dramatic quality, were taken up into them. There came into being a true popular drama, quick with possibilities. On the other hand, most fortunately, separate and apart from this popular drama, there developed and grew to a characteristic strength of its own a literary drama in the university and in the court, the inspiration for which came from external sources. The native popular drama was not destined to dwindle away through being overshadowed by this literary drama, for this literary drama existed in a world apart. Sooner or later, while the literary drama continued to develop in its separate sphere, its influence had to reach the popular drama, and there by interfusion produce a higher form which partook of the strength of both. But this higher form was not a stage in the development of the literary drama. It was a stage in the development of the popular drama. It was a professional drama, its plays were invented or adapted for professional use, and they were played by professional actors. In brief, the balance of strength lay always with the popular drama, for however the literary drama, drawing on its external sources of inspiration, might grow in strength, its acquirement must inevitably in time pass down to the popular drama, from which, however, it derived little in turn.

Our next duty is to consider this literary or learned drama, to see whence it came, and the manner in which it influenced the popular drama.

IX

THE THREE ARTISTIC IMPULSES IN ELIZABETHAN DRAMA

Three artistic impulses may be discerned as shaping the drama. The first of these, the humanistic or " classical " impulse, is foreign and purely scholarly. The second, the " romantic " impulse, is inherent in dramatic inspiration, but in our drama received a special form and direction from foreign sources. The third, the impulse towards realism, is inherent, and might at any time become dominant in particular works, or the works of particular men.

The humanistic, or classical, impulse took its rise in the classical plays of the universities and the schools, which included both plays written in Latin and English plays written on Latin models. Humanism — the study of the classics to apply its lessons to problems of the present, which formed so important a part of the complex movement called the Renaissance — affected the drama, as it affected all other types of literature. In the universities and the schools, plays were written on the model of the Roman playwrights, Plautus and Seneca, who were adopted as exemplars of comedy and tragedy respectively. The first true English tragedy, *Gorboduc*, was modeled on Seneca; the first true English comedy, *Ralph Roister Doister*, was modeled on Plautus. Both, it is worth noting, were written on English themes, and the one was written for the court, the other by a schoolmaster, Nicholas Udall, probably for presentation at Eton. In addition to these imitations of Seneca and Plautus, there were didactic and satirical plays, ranging from the utmost academic seriousness to delightful humor, in good part translated from, or written under the inspiration of, Continental humanists. Examples of these are Thomas Ingeland's *Disobedient Child*, Gascoigne's *Glass of Government*, and (far removed from these in kind and date) *Pedantius* and *Ignoramus*. The inspiration derived from this classical influence was the attempt to attain a formal ideal, and its appeal was to things familiar and hallowed by association with the past. In its narrower range of the formal academic drama, it continued into the seventeenth century and found expression in the serious plays, fine but somewhat remote from popular taste and interest,

of Greville, Daniel, and Alexander. In the broader
range of realistic humanism, its culminating value,
much modified by his individuality, was reached in
Ben Jonson, whose noble genius broadened and
further liberalized its conceptions and methods, both
in tragedy (*Sejanus, Cataline*), and in satiric comedies of " humors " (salient traits of character displayed
and emphasized in special characters), which was one
important source of the pure " comedy of manners,"
in which the customs of contemporary life were pic-
tured and heightened, whether for entertainment simply,
or with satiric intent. The comedy of manners, with
its scope of human interest greatly narrowed, with its
humor largely displaced by wit, and with no moral
basis for character assumed, as had earlier been the
case, at least tacitly, became the characteristic comedy
of the Restoration. The use of humors, as a theatrical
convention or, what is much the same thing, because
of the dramatist's barrenness of invention, where originally it was an instrument for the concentration of his
strength, constantly reappears in our drama down to
the present day.

The earlier classical influence is practically confined
to plays for the universities, the schools, and the court.
The greater playwrights who characteristically show
this influence belong to the seventeenth century, when
the separation of the literary and popular drama had
ceased to exist. In the earlier history of the popular
drama, before this had happened, the influence of Seneca had reached the popular drama in the *Spanish
Tragedy* of Kyd, which necessarily reflected the then
prevailing Senecan influence. The fact that this influence reached the popular drama (albeit Kyd's play

reflects it, especially in structural features), and through a playwright not himself apparently a university man, is significant of the inevitable gravitation of results attained by the literary drama into the popular drama, to which reference has been made above. As concerns the influence exerted by Kyd, it means little, for he represents essentially the romantic impulse.

The second impulse, that of the spirit of romance, is by far the most important. Its aim is to attract and please by something before unknown; the poet, a law unto himself, using what materials and methods he pleases, strives to embody fittingly the images of power and of beauty conceived by his freely working imagination; his appeal is through the new aspect he gives to things familiar, or through the allurement of things remote and strange in place or time. The drama which resulted from this impulse was as distinctively a Renaissance product as the humanistic classical drama, and indeed more characteristically; for, if the humanistic drama represented reference to the past for guidance, this represented the unfettered genius creating its own ideals and dominating inherited or acquired conditions or laws, that is, it represented the independence of tradition which is the very soul of the Renaissance movement. The romantic spirit in Elizabethan drama found its strength in, and took direction from, the inspiration of Italian literature in verse and prose — in lyric verse, the pastoral, the allegoric epic, and in popular fiction, the romance and short tale; also, to a lesser extent, it was indebted to Spanish literature. English playwrights drew innumerable themes from Italian literature, but, substantial gain though this in itself was, far more important was the lesson they

learned of intellectual and imaginative and artistic independence, and the inspiration they received toward
poetic conception and expression. This lesson was applied to, and guided them infallibly right in their use
of, native themes as well, whether from medieval romance (native in the sense of being the common prop-
erty of all Europe), or drawn from British history.

This romantic influence, still under limitation of its
sources, appears first in the literary drama, in the
allegorical and courtly drama of Lyly and Peele. Its
growing ascendency may be traced also in the Senecan drama and in the changed spirit of comedy; but
of supreme importance is its appearance in the work of
certain professional playwrights of the popular drama,
who indeed placed the triumph of the popular drama
over the amateur and scholarly drama beyond all doubt.
The beginning of the transformation of the popular
drama came through Kyd, who conjoined in his tragedies romantic inspiration and Senecan influence, with
the result of an immense gain in imaginative breadth
and power. Soon the far finer genius of Marlowe, university bred, uniting a superb insolence of conscious
power with a reckless arrogance of will and temper,
lent its aid in the work which Kyd had begun. With
Marlowe came a marked advance in constructive skill,
notably as regards the balance of humor and pathos;
what is more important, with him the dialogue became
magical poetry; moreover — from a dramatic standpoint, of even greater importance — he conclusively
placed the dramatic action where it belongs, namely,
within the breasts of the characters, in their motives
and passions, and not in sequence of incidents. His
characterization was, however, defective in this, that

led by his temperament he made his personages effect
ive and impressive by making them superhuman in
their attributes or powers; they are saved from abnor-
mality or unreality, and are dramatically credible, because we recognize that they are real in their motives
and passions; though enlarged to superhuman pro-
portions, their impressiveness is not due to a specious
use of an unnatural or impossible conjunction of qualities or lack of balance between qualities. The work
of Shakespeare next consummated that of Marlowe in
lifting the popular drama to the highest artistic plane.
In bald terms, he made the central dramatic essential,
the character, rational and realistic, without in the least
vulgarizing it or rendering it prosaic. He was by no
means such a master of mere constructive skill as Ben
Jonson was, for, while he recognized to the full the dramatic value of this or that incident, the very fact of his
jealousy of its worth together with the prodigality of his
powers led him occasionally to admit incidents that were,
from the standpoint of dramatic economy, non-essential
and therefore better omitted; but, on the other hand,
he brought to, and expended upon, the dialogue of the
play every utmost excellence of poetry and eloquence.
Shakespeare, as he was the supreme genius of his age,
was also its creature; he ran through every current
mode, tried his hand at all, — attained, naturally and
unconsciously, to the perfect law of liberty through
obedience. This is no place to attempt (if any one were
able) an appreciation of the height and range of his
achievement; the elevation and breadth of his comedy,
and its immortal drollery and roguishness; his plays
of mixed mode and of fantasia. But in respect to his
tragedy, one point of preëminent historical importance

must be noted. Shakespeare shares with Marlowe the peculiar glory of lifting the popular drama to the artistic plane. He, like him, took the historical play of the popular drama, the chronicle history, gave it ultimate artistic unity of plot, endowed its characterization with humanity, and transfused it with, and embodied it in, poetry. From the transformed chronicle history came in part the inspiration for the great tragedies, such as *Hamlet, Macbeth,* and *Lear* — the greatest tragedy the world has seen, because it is life substantial in its poetry and passion, imaginatively seen and rendered in terms of its realities laid bare, while the Greek tragedy, more purely poetic and artistic in its inspiration, is less life itself than a sublimated essence from the poetry and passion of life.

Our greatest plays are in the romantic mode, but this mode, in which the genius of the individual poet is everything, is also subject to defects in the individual genius and temperament. Into the decadence of the romantic inspiration among the lesser playwrights of the seventeenth century we cannot go, but we may note that, as the energy of the creative impulse slackened, the influence which remained operative was that of Fletcher. His taint of sentimentality in the presentation of characters which are paragons of virtue and of themes involving high-strained self-sacrifice, unreal and more than bordering on the insincere, reinforced by a similar sentimentality from the French romances (ultimately in part Spanish), passed through D'Avenant into the " heroic play " of Dryden and others after the Restoration, with its patterns of virtue and its conflicts between love and honor. The heroic play, essentially an artificial and temporary type, speedily ran its course, though various elements in it — its patterns of virtue, its impossibly wicked characters, its declamatory passages of moralizing, its rant and bombast, — trailed off after its dissolution among the more worthless plays of the eighteenth century, and persist under changed forms to-day.

The third artistic impulse in the Elizabethan period was that toward popular realism, the depiction in simulated actuality of contemporaneous life, or what was taken to be the life of the past. This impulse is a natural one in the drama at all periods; it appears in our drama from the interludes of John Heywood through Greene, Dekker, Thomas Heywood, and Middleton, to Brome in the reign of Charles I. The motives underlying it may be sincerely artistic or purely mercenary. Among the playwrights of the early seventeenth century are such true artists as Heywood and Dekker, and beside them men who would put anything or everything on the stage that might catch popular fancy and ensure patronage, such as Middleton and Brome.

It will be understood that there was no clear separation of the three main tendencies just indicated. In their interplay, they produced a countless variety of themes and treatments, one or another playwright at one time or another trying various modes, or combinations of modes, or modifications of various kinds. It should also be understood that in a diagrammatic outline such as this, it is not possible, in a limited space and with avoidance of confusion, to specify, to any satisfactory purpose, the place and achievement of even the greater dramatists, or still less to point out the relation to the general movement of individual plays. The intention of the outline is simply to indicate in a general way how the religious and moral drama, illus-trated in this book, developed into the Elizabethan drama. For detailed study of the subject, the reader is referred to Mr. Schelling's *Elizabethan Drama.* Of special interest, in relation to the theme of this volume, is his clear exposition of the influences of the religious and moral drama which extended down into the Eliza-bethan drama,— that, as he says, " the roots of Eliz-abethan drama lie deep in the miracles and especially in the moral plays of medieval times," and that " even the extraordinary diversity in kind and species which the later drama examples is prefigured in them."

X

METHODS USED IN TRANSLATION

A word as to the methods used in translating the plays selected for this volume. The original is followed, in respect to verse and rime, as closely as the ability of the translator permitted. Where rime or assonance (partial rime of the vowel only, like *take, mate*) fails in the original, the translation follows the omission. Very seldom, where exigency demanded it in order that the original might be reproduced more closely, an assonance is used, such as the original elsewhere uses, in place of pure rime. Where rimes on syllables with secondary stress are used in the original (as on *-ing*), these rimes are reproduced. When words not in the original are used, they are replaced, with scarcely an exception, by words then in use, and similar care has been used with occasional tags added to make the rime.

The translation of Middle English into Modern English always presents many trifling but in their way difficult problems, and such a work as the *Second Shepherds' Play*, with its complicated rime scheme, necessitates a constant succession of minor *tours de force*. Where paraphrase has been used or words are added, the fact is recorded in the notes. The translator has tried his best, in brief, to enable the reader to realize the spirit, content, and form of the original.

The reader will find difficulty at first in reading the verse as it should be read ; till he gets to understand it, it will seem more shockingly rough even than it is. It is rough in the original — may one venture to express the modest hope that it is not more than faithfully so in the translation? The secret of reading it is a loyal love for English traditions in verse, and the power to divine by some happy faculty where the strong beats come irrespective of the number of unstressed syllables between them. Mr. Saintsbury has said that he does not possess organs of speech which enable him to run lightly over three unstressed syllables before he reaches the blessed security of a strong beat. It is to be hoped there are not many so unfortunate. Such persons are confined to the mechanical neatness, simplicity, and obvious symmetry of alternate stressed and unstressed, and are blind to the history of English prosody. They must miss wholly the music of many an exquisite line of modern English verse where two or three strong beats come together, or where two strong beats are separated by more than the statutory number — they allow two — of unstressed syllables. It is a verse-deaf school of prosodists, that limits the free range of English verse

by the ultimate test of counting on the fingers. This
may seem to be going somewhat far afield from our
immediate subject, but not really so. Much of fifteenth-
century popular verse is rough, indeed often defective,
though not nearly as often so as verse written in fum-
bling or decadent imitation of foreign modes. But only
one blind to the historic facts of English prosody, deaf
to what it means of magic in modern verse, will deny
that the popular verse of this period, despite foreign
influence, is idiomatically English, and that it preserved an English tradition which to-day gives our verse
a flexibility and variety infinitely superior to the regu-
larity and monotony of the exotic rhythm over which,
while assimilating its best qualities, it triumphed.

THE ENGLISH QUEM QUÆRITIS

FROM THE REGULARIS CONCORDIA MONACHORUM

[WITH regard to the trope in general, see the *Introduction*. The *Regularis Concordia Anglicæ Nationis Monachorum*, from which this version of the *Quem Quæritis* is taken, may be best consulted in the edition of W. S. Logeman, *De Consuetudine Monachorum*, in *Anglia*, vol. xiii, 365. For critical comment and discussion of authorship and date, see in particular Logeman, *Anglia*, vol. xv, 20, F. Tupper, *Modern Language Notes*, vol. viii, 344, Chambers, *Mediæval Stage*, vol. ii, 306. The work has been accredited to Dunstan and Ælfric. The better view seems to be that of Chambers, that it was written by, or compiled under the oversight of, Ethelwold, who became Bishop of Winchester in 963. Its date falls between 965, when Elfrida, who is mentioned in the *Proœmium*, became queen, and the death of Edgar in 975, in whose reign it was compiled.

This version of the *Quem Quæritis* is of special interest because it was in use in England, because of its early date, and because of the fullness with which the ritual is given. Only the leading words of the dialogue are given, but the missing words are here supplied in brackets. The original Latin of the dialogue is retained in the translation, as elsewhere in the citations where parts of the service are quoted, but a translation is provided in the notes. It seemed desirable to give with the *Quem Quæritis* also the ceremonial of the Adoration and Deposition of the Cross, which precede it and with which it is connected. The more important parts of the original in this connection are printed by Chambers in abbreviated form in his *Appendix O ;* he gives a translation of the parts concerning the *Quem Quæritis*, vol. ii, 14–16. Manly prints both this *Quem Quæritis*, vol. i, xix, and one from two tropers originally belonging to Winchester Cathedral. The passages below will be found at pp. 416–419, 421–423, 426–428 of Logeman's edition.]

On the Parasceve [1] day [Good Friday] let Tenebræ [2] [*nocturna laus*] be performed as before described. Thereafter let all those coming to Prime [3] approach unshod until that the cross is adored. For, on that same day, at the time of Nones, [4] let the abbot go with the brethren to the church. The prayer being finished, when he shall have been vested in the usual manner, coming with the servers of the altar from the sacristy before the altar to offer prayer, let him go thence to his own seat in silence. Then let the subdeacon go up to read the lesson from the prophet Hosea, *In tribulatione sua.* Then follows the respond *Domine audivi* with four verses. Thereafter the prayer *Deus a quo et Judas* is offered by the abbot with a genuflection. Thereafter is read another lesson *Dixit Dominus ad Moysen.* The *tractus, Eripe me, Domine,* follows. Thereafter the Passion of our Lord Jesus Christ according to John is read. For this Passion let the deacon not say *Dominus vobiscum,* but *Passio Domini,* &c., no one replying *Gloria tibi, Domine.* And when there is read in the gospel *Partiti sunt vestimenta mea,* &c., forthwith let two deacons strip the altar of its covering, previously placed beneath the Gospel, doing this in the manner of one who steals.[5] Thereafter let the prayers be celebrated, and let the abbot, coming before the altar, begin the special prayers of the day which follow, and say the first without genuflection as if reading, *Oremus dilectissimi nobis*, &c. These things fulfilled in due order, let the cross forthwith be prepared before the altar, supported on either side by two deacons within the space left between it and the altar. Then let them sing *Popule meus*, but let two sub-deacons, standing before the cross, sing in response in Greek, *Agios O Theos, agios y[s]chiros, agiós athanatos, eleison ymas*. And the choir likewise that very same in Latin, *Sanctus Deus*. Let the cross then be borne by the deacons themselves before the altar, and let an acolyte follow with a cushion, upon which the holy cross may be placed. And, the antiphon finished to which the choir responds in Latin, let them sing the same as before, *Qu[i]a edux[i] vos per desertum.** Let the sub-deacons again respond in Greek as before, *Agios*, as above. And again the choir in Latin as before, *Sanctus Deus*. And let the deacons likewise, elevating the cross, sing as before, *Quid ultra*. Again the sub-deacons as before, *Agios, ut supra*. And again the choir in Latin, *Sanctus Deus*, as above. After this, turning to the priest with the cross bared, let them sing the antiphon *Ecce lignum crucis ;* and again, *Crucem tuam adoramus ;* and again, *Dum fabricator mundi ;* [and again (?)] [*P*]*ange lingua*. So soon as it is bared, let the abbot come before the holy cross, and prostrate himself thrice successively with all the breth-

* MS. (Logeman) *perde sertum.*

ren at the right side of the choir, namely the seniors
and juniors, and with great sighing of the heart let
him pray by intoning the seven penitential psalms
with the appropriate prayers of the holy cross. [Di-
rections for the psalms and accompanying prayers follow.] . . . And, kissing the cross with humility, let
him rise. Then let all the brethren at the left side of
the choir do the same with devout minds. When, indeed, the cross has been saluted by the abbot or by
all, let the abbot himself return to his seat, the while
every cleric and the people do the same thing.

For, since on this day we celebrate the deposition of
the body of our Saviour, we have decided to follow, with
close similarity, the usage of certain religious, worthy
of imitation for confirming the faith of the ignorant
vulgar and of neophytes — if so it should have seemed
good to any one, or in such wise have pleased him
— in the manner following.[6] Let there be, indeed,
in a part of the altar which is bare, some sort of a
representation of the sepulchre and a veil of some
kind drawn about it, in which let the holy cross, when
it has been adored, be deposited with the following
ceremonial. Let the deacons who before bore it come
and wind it in linen in the place where it was adored.
Then let them carry it back, singing the antiphon *In
pace in id ipsum habitabit,* also *Caro mea requiescet
in spe,* until they come to the place of the tomb [*mo-
numento,* read *monumenti*], and the cross being deposited as if it were the buried body of our Lord
Jesus Christ, let them say the antiphon *Sepulto do-
mino, signatum est monumentum, ponentes milites qui
custodirent eum.* Let the holy cross be guarded with
all reverence in this same place until the Sunday night

of his resurrection. At night, indeed, let two brothers, or three, or more if there shall be so large a gathering, be appointed, to observe faithful vigils there by singing psalms. These things done, let the deacon and sub-deacon enter from the sacristy with the body of the Lord which remained from the day before and with a chalice with unconsecrated wine, and let them place it upon the altar, &c. [The Mass of the Pre-sancti-fied⁷ follows, followed by the services of Easter Eve.] ... During the same night [of Easter Eve], before the bells of Matins are rung, let the sacristans take up the cross and set it in some suitable place. First in the Nocturnes, when the praise of God is begun in the church by the abbot or some priest, let him say *Labia mea aperies* once only, and the *Deus in adiutorium meum intende* with the *Gloria*. Then, the psalm *Domine, quid multiplicati sunt*, being omitted, let the cantor begin the Invitatory. Then the three antiphons with the three psalms. These finished, let a fitting verse be said, then as many lessons with the responds pertaining rightly thereunto.

While the third lesson is being chanted, let four brothers vest themselves, one of whom, vested in an alb, enters as if to do something, and, in an inconspicuous way, approaches the place where the sepulchre is, and there, holding a palm in his hands, sits quiet. While the third respond is chanted, let the three others approach, all alike vested in copes, bearing thuribles⁸ with incense in their hands, and, with hesitating steps, in the semblance of persons seeking something, let them come before the place of the sepulchre. These things are done, indeed, in representation of the angel sitting within the tomb and of the

women who came with spices to anoint the body of
Jesus. When, therefore, he who is seated sees the
three approaching as if wandering about and seeking
something, let him begin to sing melodiously and in a
voice moderately loud, *Quem quœritis* [*in sepulchro,
O Christicolœ?*].⁹ When_this has been sung to the
end, let the three respond in unison, *Iesum Nazare-
num* [*crucifixum, O cœlicola*]. Then he, *Non est hic.
Surrexit, sicut prœdixerat. Ite, nuntiate quia surrexit a mortuis.* Upon the utterance of this command,
let the three turn to the choir and say, *Alleluia, resur-
rexit Dominus!* This said, let him, still remaining
seated, say as if calling them back, the antiphon *Venite,
et videte locum* [*ubi positus erat Dominus. Alleluia, Alleluia!*]. Having said this, however, let him
rise and lift the veil, and show them the place empty
of the cross, but the cloths, only, laid there with
which the cross was wrapped. When they see this,
let them set down the thuribles that they have carried
within that same sepulchre, and take up the cloth and
hold it up before the clergy, and, as if in testimony
that the Lord has risen and is not now wrapped
therein, let them sing this antiphon : *Surrexit Dominus de sepulchro* [*qui pro nobis pependit in ligno*],
and let them lay the cloth upon the altar. The antiphon finished, let the prior, rejoicing with them in the
triumph of our King, in that, death vanquished, he
has risen, begin the hymn *Te Deum laudamus.* This
begun, all the bells are rung together, at the end of
which let the priest say the verse, *In resurrectione tua,
Christe,* as far as this word, and let him begin Matins
[read *Lauds*], saying, *Deus, in adiutorium meum
intende,* &c.

THE BROME ABRAHAM AND ISAAC

[THE translation is based upon Manly's edition in his *Specimens of the Pre-Shaksperean Drama*, and the editions of Miss Lucy Toulmin Smith, upon which his edition was based, in *Anglia*, vol. vii, 316–337, and *A Commonplace Book of the Fifteenth Century*. . . . *Printed from the Original MS. at Brome Hall, Suffolk, by Lady Caroline Kerrison. Edited with Notes by Lucy Toulmin Smith. London and Norwich*, 1886. Local entries in the commonplace book, in which the play was found, date from 1499. The play probably dates from about 1470 or 1480. Of the five extant plays on its theme, no one approaches it in the natural dramatic feeling with which the pathos of the situation is brought out; the change of Isaac's mood, most charming and touching, to childish gayety and sportiveness when his death is averted is particularly striking. The play which most nearly equals it in quality is the Dublin version, published by J. P. Collier, *Five Miracle Plays*, 1836. For a description of the MS., see the article in *Anglia, ut supra*. Emendations are suggested by Holthausen, *Anglia*, vol. xiii, 361.]

[Abraham and Isaac enter.]
Abraham.

Father of Heaven, omnipotent,
  With all my heart to thee I call,
Thou hast given me both land and rent,
And my livelihood thou hast to me sent,
  I thank thee greatly evermore for all.

First of the earth thou madest Adam,
   And Eve also to be his wife ;
All other creatures from these two came:
And now thou has granted me, Abraham,
   Here in this land to lead my life.   **10**

In mine age thou hast granted me this
   That with me should dwell this young child dear.
I love nothing so much, ywis,
Except thine own self, dear Father of Bliss,
   As my own sweet son, my Isaac here.   **15**

I have divers children more, I know,
   But I love them not half so well as he.
This fair sweet child he doth cherish me so,
In every place wherever I go,
   That no affliction may trouble me.   **20**

And therefore, Father of Heaven, I thee pray
   For his health and also for his grace.
Now, Lord, keep him both night and day
That never affliction nor terror may
   Come to my child in any place.   **25**

Now come on, Isaac, my own sweet child,
   Go we home and take our rest.

           Isaac.

Abraham, mine own father so mild,
   To follow you I am readiest
     Late and early, God wot !   **30**

         Abraham.

Come on, sweet child, I love thee best
   Of all the children that ever I begot.

[Abraham and Isaac go. God speaks :]
            Deus.

Mine angel, fast hie thee on thy way,
    And unto mid-earth anon do thou go —
Abraham's heart now will I essay,   35
    Whether he be stedfast or no.

Say I commanded him for to take
    His young son Isaac, he loveth so,
And with his blood that he sacrifice make
    If my friendship he would have and know.   40

Show him the way unto the hill
    Where that his sacrifice shall be.
I shall essay now his good will,
    Whether he loveth better his child or me.
All men shall take example by him   45
    My commandments how they shall keep.

[The Angel goes to find Abraham. Abraham speaks :]
            Abraham.

Now, Father of Heaven, that didst form everything,
    My prayers I make to thee again,
For this day my tender offering
    Here must I give to thee amain.   50

Ah, Lord God, Almighty King,
    What kind will be to thee most fain?
If I had thereof true knowing,
    It should be done with might and main
        Full soon by me!   55
To do thy pleasure on a hill,
Verily, it is my will,
    Dear Father, God in Trinity!

[The Angel appears to Abraham.]
The Angel.

Abraham, Abraham, be at rest!
   Our Lord commandeth thee to take   60
Isaac, thy young son, that thou lovest best
   And with his blood that thou sacrifice make.

Into the Land of Vision do thou go,
   And offer thy child unto thy Lord ;
I shall thee lead and show also.   65
   To God's bidding, Abraham, give accord,

And follow me upon this green !
Abraham.
   Welcome to me be my Lord's command !
   And his behest I will not withstand —
   Yet Isaac, my young son in land,   70
A full dear child to me hath been !

Were God so pleased, I were liefer rid
   Of all the good that I have, he gave,
Than that Isaac, my son, were discomforted,
   So God in heaven my soul may save !   75

No thing on earth so much love I bore,
   And now I must the child go kill !
Ah, Lord God, my conscience is troubled sore,
And yet, my dear Lord, I dread me the more
   To begrudge anything against thy will.   80

I love my child as my life,
   But yet I love my God much more thereto,
For though my heart should make any strife,
Yet will I not spare for child or wife,
   But do as my Lord hath bid me do !   85

Though I love my son never so great a deal,
  Yet smite off his head soon I shall.
Ah, Father of Heaven, to thee I kneel,
A hard death my son shall feel,
  For to honor thee, Lord, withal!   90

The Angel.
Abraham, Abraham, this is well said,
  And all these decrees look thou obey!
But in thy heart be nothing dismayed.
                Abraham.
Nay, nay, forsooth! I hold me well paid
  To please my God the best I may.   95

For though my heart be in heaviness set
  The blood of my own dear son to see,
Yet will I not withhold my debt,
But Isaac, my son, I will go get,
  And come as fast as ever may be.   100

[*The Angel departs. Abraham goes to fetch Isaac :*]
                Abraham.
Now, Isaac, my own son dear,
  Where art thou, child! Speak to me.
                Isaac.
My fair sweet father, I am here,
  And make my prayers to the Trinity.

                Abraham.
Rise up, my child, and fast come hither,   105
  My gentle bairn that art so wise,
For we too, child, must go together,
  And unto my Lord make sacrifice.

Isaac.

I am full ready, my father. Lo!
  Given to your hands, I stand right here,   110
And whatsoever ye bid me do, even so
  It shall be done with glad cheer,
      Full well and fine.

Abraham.

Ah, Isaac, mine own son so dear,
  God's blessing I give thee, and mine.   115

Hold this fagot upon thy back,
  And I myself here fire shall bring.

Isaac.

Father, all this here will I pack,
  I am full fain to do your bidding.

Abraham.

Ah, Lord of Heaven, my hands I wring,   120
This child's words wound like death my heart!

Now, Isaac, son, go we on our way
  Unto yon mount with might and main.

Isaac.

Let us go, my dear father, as fast as I may —
  To follow you I am full fain,   125
      Although I be slender.

Abraham.

Ah, Lord, my heart breaketh in twain,
  This child's words, they be so tender!

Ah, Isaac son, anon lay it there,
  No longer upon thy back it hold,   130
For I must make ready prayer
  To honor my Lord God as I was told.

Isaac.

Lo, my dear father, where it is.
   To cheer you, always I draw me near,
But, father, I marvel sore at this,   135
   Why it is that ye make this heavy cheer,

And also, father, ever more fear I —
   Where is your quick beast that ye should kill?
Both fire and wood we have ready by,
   But quick beast have we none on this hill.   140

A quick beast, I wot well, slain must be,
   Your sacrifice to make.

Abraham.

Dread thee not, my child, I counsel thee
Our Lord will unto this place send me
   Some manner of beast to take   145
      By his sweet command.

Isaac.

Yea, father, but my heart beginneth to quake
   To see that sharp sword in your hand.

Why bear ye your sword drawn so?
   Of your countenance I have much wonder!   150

Abraham.

Ah, Father of Heaven, so great is my woe,
   This child here breaks my heart in sunder.

Isaac.

Tell me, my dear father, ere that ye cease —
   Bear ye your sword thus drawn for me?

Abraham.

Ah, Isaac, sweet son, peace, peace!   155
   For in sooth thou breakest my heart in three!

Isaac.

Now truly, father, on somewhat ye think,
　That ye mourn thus more and more.

Abraham.

Ah, Lord of Heaven, let thy grace down sink,
　For my heart was never half so sore!　　　　160

Isaac.

I pray you, father, let me know the truth,
　Whether I shall have any harm or no.

Abraham.

Not yet may I tell thee, sweet son, in sooth,
　My heart is now so full of woe.

Isaac.

Dear father, I pray you, hide it not from me,　165
　But some of your thought, tell ye me, your son.

Abraham.

Ah, Isaac, Isaac, I must kill thee!

Isaac.

Kill me, father? Alas, what have I done!

If in aught I have trespassed against you, God wot,
　With a rod ye may make me full mild —　　170
And with your sharp sword kill me not,
　For in truth, father, I am but a child.

Abraham.

I am full sorry, son, thy blood to spill,
　But truly, my child, it is not as I please.

Isaac.

Now I would to God my mother were here on this hill!
　Sh——— ——— neel for me on both her knees　175
　　　　To save my life.

And since that my mother is not here,
Change your look, I pray you, father dear,
 And kill me not with your knife.   180

Abraham.

Forsooth, my son, save I thee kill,
 I should grieve God right sore, I fear,
It is his commandment and also his will
 That I should do this same deed here.

He commanded me, son, for certain   185
 To make my sacrifice with thy blood.

Isaac.

And is it God's will that I should be slain?

Abraham.

Yea, truly, Isaac, my son so good,
 And therefore my hands I wring!

Isaac.

Now, father, against my Lord's decree, 190
 I will never murmur, loud or still.
He might have sent me a better destiny,
 If it had been his will.

Abraham.

Forsooth, son, save this deed I did,
 In grievous displeasure our Lord would be. 195

Isaac.

Nay, nay, father, God forbid
 That ever ye should grieve him for me!

Ye have other children, one or two,
 Which ye should love well in natural kind.
I pray you, father, no more your grief renew, 200
For, if I am once dead and gone from you,
 I shall soon be out of your mind.

Therefore do our Lord's bidding,
　And when I am dead, then pray for me.
But, good father, tell ye my mother nothing,　　205
Say that I am in another country dwelling.

Abraham.

　Ah, Isaac, Isaac, blessed mayest thou be!

My heart in anguish beginneth to rise
　To see the blood of thy blessed body!

Isaac.

Father, since it may be no other wise,　　210
　Let it pass over, as well as I.

But, father, ere I go unto my death,
　I pray you bless me with your hand.

Abraham.

Now, Isaac, with all my breath,
　My blessing I give thee upon this land,　　215
　　And, verily, God's thereto with this.
Isaac, Isaac, son, rise up and stand,
　　Thy fair sweet mouth that I may kiss.

Isaac.

Now farewell, my own father so fine,
　And greet well my mother as may accord,　　220
But I pray you, father, to hide mine eyne
　That I see not the stroke of your sharp sword
　　That my flesh shall defile.

Abraham.

Son, thy words make me to weep full sore —
Now, my dear son Isaac, speak no more.　　225

Isaac.

Ah, my own dear father, wherefore?
　We shall speak here together so little while.

And since tnat I must needs be dead,
　Yet, my dear father, to you I pray,
Smite but few strokes at my head   230
　And make an end as soon as ye may,
　　And tarry not too long.

Abraham.

Child, thy meek words do me dismay,
　So welaway must be my song!

Except alone that I do God's will.   235
　Ah, Isaac, my own sweet child,
Kiss me yet again upon this hill —
　In all the world is none so mild!

Isaac.

Now, truly, father, all this tarrying,
　It doeth my heart but harm;   240
I pray you, father, make an ending.

Abraham.

Come up, sweet child, into my arm.

I must bind thy hands two,
　Although thou be never so mild.

Isaac.

Ah, mercy, father! Why should ye so do?   245

Abraham.

That thou should'st not resist, my child.

Isaac.

Nay, indeed, father, I 'll not try to let [1] you.
  Do on, for all me, your will,   ·
And the purpose to which ye have set you,
  For God's love, hold it steadfast still.   250

I am full sorry this day to die,
  But yet I wish not my God to grieve.
Do your pleasure for all me full boldly,
  My fair sweet father, I give you leave.

But, father, I pray you evermore,   255
  Nothing unto my mother tell,
If she knew it, she would weep full sore,
  For she loveth me, father, in truth, full well —
    May God's blessing with her be!
Now farewell, my mother so sweet,   260
We two are like no more to meet,

Abraham.

Ah, Isaac, Isaac, son, thou dost make me greet,
  And with thy words thou doth anguish me!

Isaac.

I am sorry, sweet father, to grieve you truly;
  I cry you mercy for what I have done;   265
And for all trespass I did you unduly,
  Forgive me, dear father, all I have done.
    God of Heaven be with me!

Abraham.

Ah, dear child, forbear to moan!
In all thy life, thou didst grieve me none.   270
Now blessed be thou, body and bone,

---

[1] Prevent.

That ever thou wert bred and born.
Thou hast been to me a child full good.
  But in truth, child, though I mourn,
     Never so fast,[1]
  Yet must I needs here at the last   275
In this place shed all thy blood.

Therefore, my dear son, here shalt thou lie.
  Unto my work I must proceed.
In truth, I as lief were myself should die —
  If God would be pleased with my deed —   280
    And mine own body for to offer!
           Isaac.
Ah, mercy, father! mourn ye no more.
Your weeping maketh mine heart as sore
  As mine own death I am to suffer.

Your kerchief, father, about mine eyes wind.   285
           Abraham.
  So I shall, sweetest child on earth so broad.
           Isaac.
Now still, good father, have this in mind,
  And smite me not often with your sharp sword,
    But hastily that it be sped.
Here Abraham laid a cloth on Isaac's face, thus saying :
           Abraham.
Now farewell, my child so full of grace !   290
           Isaac.
Ah, father, father, turn downward my face !
  For of your sharp sword I am ever adread.

           Abraham.
To do this deed I am full sorry,
  But, Lord, thy behest I will not withstand.

[1] See note with regard to the numbering of the lines.

Isaac.

Ah, Father of Heaven, to thee I cry.   295
   Lord, receive me into thy hand!

Abraham.

Lo, now is the time come for sure
   That my sword into his neck shall bite.
Ah, Lord, my heart may not this endure,
   I may not find it in my heart to smite!   300
      My heart is not equal thereunto!
'Yet fain would I work my Lord's will,
But this young innocent lieth so still,
I may not find it in my heart him to kill —
      O Father of Heaven, what shall I do!   305

Isaac.

Ah, mercy, father, why tarry ye so,
   And let me so long on this heath thus lie?
Now I would God the stroke were no more to know.
Father, heartily I pray you, shorten my woe,
   And let me not wait thus, looking to die.   310

Abraham.

Now, heart, why would'st thou not break in thee?
   Yet shált thou not máke me to my Gód unmild.
I will no longer hold back for thee,
Because that my God would offended be.
   Now receive the stroke, my own dear child.   315

Here Abraham drew his stroke, and the Angel took the
sword in his hand suddenly.
The Angel.
I am an angel, thou mayest quickly soon see,
   That from heaven to thee is sent.

Our Lord a hundred times thanketh thee
  For the keeping of his commandment.
He knoweth thy will and also thine heart,   320
  That thou fearest him above everything,
And to ease of thy heaviness a part,
  A fair ram yonder I did bring.

Lo, among the briars he standeth tied.
  Now, Abraham, amend thy mood,   325
For Isaac, thy young son, here by thy side,
  This day shall not shed his blood.
Go, make thy sacrifice with yon ram.
Now farewell, blessed Abraham,
For unto heaven I go now home: 330
  The way is full straight.
    Take up thy son so free!

                                          [*The Angel goes.*

                    Abraham.

Ah, Lord, I thank thee for thy great grace,
  Now am I eased in divers wise.
    Arise up, Isaac, my dear son, arise,   335
Arise up, sweet child, and come to me!

                    Isaac.

Ah, mercy, father, why do ye not smite?
  Ah, smite on, father, once with your knife!

                    Abraham.

Peace, my sweet son, let your heart be light,
  For our Lord of Heaven hath granted thy life   340
    By his angel now,

That thou shalt not die this day, son, truly.

Isaac.

Ah, father, full glad then were I,
   Iwis,[1] father, I say, iwis,
      If this tale were true!   245

Abraham.

A hundred times, my son fair of hue,
   For joy thy mouth now will I kiss.

Isaac.

Ah, my dear father Abraham,
   Will not God be wroth that we do thus?

Abraham.

No, no, surely, my sweet son! for yon same ram[2] 350
   He hath sent hither down to us.

Yon beast shall die here in thy stead,
   In honor of our Lord, alone!
Go fetch him hither, my child, indeed.   355

Isaac.

Father, I will go catch him by the head,
   And bring yon beast with me anon.

Ah, sheep, sheep, blessed may thou be!
   That ever thou wert sent down hither!
Thou shalt this day die for me,   360
In worship of the Holy Trinity.
   Now come fast and go we together,
      To my father quick hie!
Though thou be never so gentle and good,
Yet I had liefer thou should'st shed thy blood,   365
   In sooth, sheep, than I!

[1] For certain, truly.
[2] See note as regards the numbering of the lines.

Lo, father, I have brought here, full smart,
  This gentle sheep, and him to you I give,
But, Lord God, I thank thee with all my heart,
  For I am glad that I shall live,   370
    And kiss again once my dear mother!

Abraham.

Now be right merry, my sweet child,
For this quick beast that is so mild,
  Here I shall offer before all other.

Isaac.

And I will fast begin to blow,   375
  This fire shall burn a full good speed,
But, father, if I stoop down low,
Ye will not kill me with your sword, I trow?

Abraham.

  No, to fear, sweet son, thou hast surely no need.
    My mourning is past!   380

Isaac.

  Yea, but I would that sword were in a fire, indeed,
    For, father, it maketh me full sore aghast!

*Here Abraham made his offering, kneeling and saying
thus :*

Abraham.

Now, Lord God of Heaven in Trinity,
  Almighty God omnipotent,
My offering I make in worship of thee,   385
  And with this quick beast I thee present.
  Lord, receive thou my intent,
As thou art God and ground of our grace.

Deus.

Abraham, Abraham, well mayest thou speed,
And Isaac, thy young son, thee by!   390

Truly, Abraham, for this deed,
 I shall multiply of you both the seed,
 As thick as stars be in the sky,
  Both of greater and less,
And as thick as the sand is in the sea, **395**
So thick multiplied your seed shall be,
 This grant I you for your goodness.

Of you shall come increase great enow,
 And ever be in bliss without end,
For me, as God alone, ye avow **400**
In fear, and to my commandments bow,
 My blessing I give wheresoever ye wend!

Abraham.

Lo, of this work that we have wrought,
 Isaac, my son, how think ye still?
Full glad and blithe may we be in thought **405**
 That we murmured not against God's will
  On this fair heath here!

Isaac.

Ah, father, I thank our Lord heartily,
That so well my wit hath served me,
 The Lord God more than my death to fear. **410**

Abraham.

Why, dearworthy son, wert thou frighted so?
 Full boldly, child, tell me thy lore.

Isaac.

By my faith, yea, father, — if aught I know,
 I was never so afraid before,
  As I have been on yon hill! **415**

But, by my faith, father, I swear
I will nevermore come there,
　　Except it be against my will!

Abraham.

Yea, come on, my own sweet son, even so,
And homeward fast now let us go.　　　　　　　　420
　　　　　　　Isaac.

　By my faith, father, thereto I agree!
I had never such good will to go home,
And to speak with my dear mother!
　　　　　　　Abraham.

　Ah, Lord of Heaven, I thank thee!
For now I may lead home with me　　　　　　425
　Isaac, my young son so free,
The gentlest child above all other,
　This may I avow full heartily.

Now, go we forth, my blessed son.
　　　　　　　Isaac.

I assent, father, and let us go,　　　　　　　430
For, by my troth, once home, why then,
I would never go out like this again.
I pray God give us grace evermore anew,
And all those that we be beholden to!

　　[Abraham and Isaac go. The Doctor enters.]
　　　　　　　Doctor.

Lo, now, sovereigns and sirs, we have showed for
　　　example　　　　　　　　　　　　　　　435
　This solemn story to great and small,
It is a good lesson for learned and simple,
　And for the wisest of us all,
　　　　　Without whipping, God wot!

For this story showeth you clear   440
How to our full power here,
    We should keep God's commandments and murmur
        not.

Think ye, sirs, if God sent an angel,
    And commanded you your child to slay,
By your truth, is there any of you   445
    That would either repine or rebel straightway?
How think ye now, sirs? I think there be
    Three or four or more hereby —
And these women that weep so sorrowfully
    When that their children from them die   450
        (As is law of kind).
It is but folly, ye well may trow,
Against God to murmur or grief to show,
For ye shall never see him mischiefed, well I know!
    By land or water, bear this in mind!   455

And murmur not against our Lord God,
    In wealth or woe, whatsoever he send,
Though low ye be bowed beneath his rod,
    For when he so willeth, he may it amend,
If his commandments with true hearts ye keep without
        fail,   460
    As this story may serve you to show and forewarn,
And him faithfully serve, while ye be sound and hale,
    That ye may please God both even and morn.
    Now Jesu, that wore the crown of thorn,
        Bring us all to heaven's bliss!   465

FINIS.

THE SECOND SHEPHERDS' PLAY

FROM THE TOWNELEY CYCLE

[THE SECOND SHEPHERDS' PLAY, justly famous for its intrinsic merit and historical importance (as already explained in the *Introduction*), derives its name from the fact that it is the second of two "Shepherds'" or Nativity plays in the Towneley, or Wakefield, cycle. It has been printed by William Marriott, 1838, the Surtees Society, 1836 (the name of the editor is not given); by England, with notes by Pollard, in the Publications of the *Early English Text Society*, 1897; separately in part by Pollard in his *English Miracle Plays, Moralities, and Interludes* (3d edition, 1898); with critical revision and with helpful emendations by Manly in his *Specimens of the Pre-Shaksperean Drama*, 1897; by Hemingway in *English Nativity Plays, Yale Studies in English*, 38, 1909; in "*Everyman*" *with other Interludes including Eight Miracle Plays*, "Everyman's Library" (no date given; general editor, Ernest Rhys; names of editors or translators of the individual plays not given). The best text for the student's use, presenting a critical interpretation of the standard text of England, is Manly's. Though Professor Manly's notes, to be included in the forthcoming third volume, are not yet published, his text itself clarifies, or at least aids the student by recording a definite opinion upon, various difficult passages. A number remain dubious, or unsolved, the solution of

which will be welcomed. Pollard's notes, while sometimes helpful, are few and only upon the special portions which he prints ; Hemingway's notes are confined
to literary and general comment. A word of warning
is necessary in regard to the marginal glosses in the
edition in "Everyman's Library," which are in many
cases curiously in error.

References to England's edition are designated
"*E. E. T. S. ;*" those to Kölbing are to his articles
in *Englische Studien*, vol. xvi, 278, vol. xxi, 162;
those to Kittredge are to his emendations and sugges-
tions in Manly's edition, as general editor of the series
in which it appeared.

The source of the story of Mak was probably a
folk-tale. Kölbing (see *E. E. T. S.* Appendix to *Introduction*, p. xxxi) pointed out features of similarity
in a rimed narrative, *Archie Armstrang's Aith*, by the
Reverend John Marriott, published in Scott's *Min-
strelsy of the Scottish Border*. Pollard in a foot-note
suggests that John Marriott may have been a relation
of William Marriott who printed the *Second Shepherds' Play* in 1838, and may therefore have known
the play and plagiarized it, even though he said the
story was traditional and at the time current in Esk-
dale. This, however. is improbable (the difference of
thirty-six years between the two is worth noting).
As Kölbing says regarding the possibility of forgery,
"It is much more credible that this funny tale was preserved by oral traditions, possibly in a metrical form.
The tale was first brought into the Christmas story by
the author of the Towneley Play, and afterwards, in the
seventeenth century, transferred to the famous thief
and jester, Archie Armstrang." The similarities and

differences between the versions, it may be added, are
of interest, but not of importance.]

[*The First Shepherd (Primus Pastor) enters.*]
Primus Pastor.

Lord, but this weather is cold, and I am ill wrapped!
Nigh dazed, were the truth told, so long have I napped;
My legs under me fold; my fingers are chapped —
With such like I don't hold, for I am all lapt
In sorrow.   5
In storms and tempest,
Now in the east, now in the west,
Woe is him has never rest
Midday nor morrow!

But we seely [1] shepherds that walk on the moor,   10
In faith we're nigh at hand to be put out of door.
No wonder, as it doth stand, if we be poor,
For the tilth of our land lies fallow as the floor,
As ye ken.
We're so burdened and banned,   15
Over-taxed and unmanned,
We're made tame to the hand
Of these gentry men.

Thus they rob us of our rest, our Lady them harry!
These men bound to their lords' behest, they make the
plough tarry,   20
What men say is for the best, we find the contrary, —
Thus are husbandmen oppressed, in point to miscarry,
In life,
Thus hold they us under

---

[1] Blameless and to be pitied; "poor."

And from comfort sunder.   25
It were great wonder,
   If ever we should thrive.

For if a man may get an embroidered sleeve or a
  brooch now-a-days,
Woe is him that may him grieve, or a word in answer
  says!
No blame may he receive, whatever pride he displays; 30
And yet may no man believe one word that he says,
   Not a letter.
His daily needs are gained
By boasts and bragging feigned,
And in all he 's maintained   35
   By men that are greater.

Proud shall come a swain as a peacock may go,
He must borrow my wain, my plough also,
Then I am full fain to grant it ere he go.
Thus live we in pain, anger, and woe   40
   By night and day!
He must have it, if he choose,
Though I should it lose,
I were better hanged than refuse,
   Or once say him nay!   45

It does me good as I walk thus alone
Of this world for to talk and to make my moan.
To my sheep will I stalk, and hearken anon,
There wait on a balk,[1] or sit on a stone.
   Full soon,   50
For I trow, pardie,

   [1] A ridge or hillock.

True men if they be,
We shall have company,
       Ere it be noon.

[*The First Shepherd goes out (or to one side). The Second*
         Shepherd enters.]
       Secundus Pastor.

Ben'cite [1] and Dominus! What may this mean?   55
Why fares the world thus! The like often we 've seen!
Lord, but it is spiteful and grievous, this weather so
    keen!
And the frost so hideous — it waters mine een!
        That's no lie!
Now in dry, now in wet,   60
Now in snow, now in sleet,
When my shoes freeze to my feet,
        It 's not all easy!

But so far as I ken, wherever I go,
We seely wedded men suffer mickle woe,   65
We have sorrow once and again, it befalls oft so.
Seely Capel, our hen, both to and fro
        She cackles,
But if she begins to croak,
To grumble or cluck,   70
Then woe be to our cock,
        For he is in the shackles! [2]

These men that are wed have not all their will;
When they 're full hard bestead, they sigh mighty still;

[1] Shortened form of *benedicite* — " bless you! " — frequent in mediæval use both as a salutation and exclamation (compare modern " bless
us ! ").

[2] I. e. in a tight place, under constraint to take what he gets.

God knows the life they are led is full hard and full
   ill,   75

Nor thereof in bower or bed may they speak their will,
                       This tide.

My share I have found,
Know my lesson all round,
Wo is him that is bound,   80
          For he must it abide!

But now late in men's lives (such a marvel to me
That I think my heart rives such wonders to see,
How that destiny drives that it should so be!)
Some men will have two wives and some men three 85
              In store.

Some are grieved that have any,
But I 'll wager my penny
Woe is him that has many,
             For he feels sore!   90

But young men as to wooing, for God's sake that you
      bought,
Beware well of wedding, and hold well in thought,
" Had I known " is a thing that serves you nought.
Much silent sorrowing has a wedding home brought,
             And grief gives,   95
With many a sharp shower —
For thou mayest catch in an hour
What shall taste thee full sour
           As long as one lives!

For — if ever read I epistle! — I have one by my
      fire,[1]   100

          [1] See note.

As sharp as a thistle, as rough as a briar,
She has brows like a bristle and a sour face by her;
If she had once wet her whistle, she might sing clearer
       and higher
              Her pater-noster;
She is as big as a whale,   105
She has a gallon of gall, —
By him that died for us all,
       I wish I had run till I had lost her!

          Primus Pastor.

"God look over the row!" like a deaf man ye stand.
          Secundus Pastor.
Yea, sluggard, the devil thy maw burn with his
       brand!   110
Didst see aught of Daw?
          Primus Pastor.
                  Yea, on the pasture-land
I heard him blow just before; he comes nigh at hand
             Below there.
Stand still.
          Secundus Pastor.
          Why?
          Primus Pastor.
For he comes, hope I.   115
          Secundus Pastor.
He 'll catch us both with some lie
          Unless we beware.

[*The Third Shepherd enters, at first without seeing them.*]
          Tertius Pastor.
Christ's cross me speed and St. Nicholas!
Thereof in sooth I had need, it is worse than it was.

Whoso hath knowledge, take heed, and let the world
    pass,   120
You may never trust .it, indeed, — it's as brittle as
    glass,
           As it rangeth.
Never before fared this world so,
With marvels that greater grow,
Now in weal, now in woe,   125
          And everything changeth.

There was never since Noah's flood such floods seen,
Winds and rains so rude and storms so keen ;
Some stammered, some stood in doubt, as I ween. —
Now God turn all to good, I say as I mean!   130
          For ponder
How these floods all drown
Both in fields and in town,
And bear all down,
          And that is a wonder!   135

We that walk of nights our cattle to keep,
          [Catches sight of the others.
We see startling sights when other men sleep.
Yet my heart grows more light — I see shrews [1] a-peep.
Ye are two tall wights — I will give my sheep
          A turn, below.   140
But my mood is ill-sent ; [2]
As I walk on this bent, [3]
I may lightly repent,
          If I stub my toe.

[1] Rascals.
[2] See note.
[3] Unenclosed pasture, heath ; a Northern use.

Ah, Sir, God you save and my master sweet!   145
A drink I crave, and somewhat to eat.

Primus Pastor.

Christ's curse, my knave, thou 'rt a lazy cheat!

Secundus Pastor.

Lo, the boy lists to rave! Wait till later for meat,
   We have eat it.
Ill thrift on thy pate!   150
Though the rogue came late,
Yet is he in state
   To eat, could he get it.

Tertius Pastor.

That such servants as I, that sweat and swink,[1]
Eat our bread full dry gives me reason to think.   155
Wet and weary we sigh while our masters wink,[2]
Yet full late we come by our dinner and drink —
   But soon thereto
Our dame and sire,
When we've run in the mire,   160
Take a nip from our hire,
   And pay slow as they care to.

But hear my oath, master, since you find fault this
   way,
I shall do this hereafter — work to fit my pay;
I'll do just so much, sir, and now and then play,   165
For never yet supper in my stomach lay
   In the fields.
But why dispute so?
Off with staff I can go.
"Easy bargain," men say,   170
   "But a poor return yields."

[1] Toil.   [2] Sleep.

Primus Pastor.

Thou wert an ill lad for work to ride wooing
From a man that had but little for spending.

Secundus Pastor.

Peace, boy, I bade! No more jangling,
Or I 'll make thee full sad, by the Heaven's King,   175
　　　　With thy gauds! [1]
Where are our sheep, boy? Left lorn? [2]

Tertius Pastor.

Sir, this same day at morn,
I them left in the corn
　　　　When they rang Lauds. [3]   180

They have pasture good, they cannot go wrong.

Primus Pastor.

That is right. By the Rood, these nights are long!
Ere we go now, I would someone gave us a song.

Secundus Pastor.

So I thought as I stood, to beguile us along.

Tertius Pastor.
　　　　I agree.   185

Primus Pastor.

The tenor I 'll try.

Secundus Pastor.

And I the treble so high.

Tertius Pastor.

Then the mean shall be I.
　　　　How ye chant now, let's see!
　　　[*They sing (the song is not given).*]

Tunc entrat Mak, in clamide se super togam vestitus. [4]

---

[1] Pranks, tricks, jokes.　　　[2] Lost.

[3] The first of the canonical hours of daily service.

[4] Then enters Mak, who has put on a cloak above his ordinary dress.

Mak.

Now, Lord, by thy seven names' spell, that made both
    moon and stars on high, 190
Full more than I can tell, by thy will for me, Lord,
    lack I.
I am all at odds, nought goes well — that oft doth my
    temper try.
Now would God I might in heaven dwell, for there no
    children cry,
            So still.

Primus Pastor.

Who is that pipes so poor? 195

Mak.

Would God ye knew what I endure!

[*Primus Pastor.*]

Lo, a man that walks on the moor,
        And has not all his will!

Secundus Pastor.

Mak, whither dost speed? What news do you bring?

Tertius Pastor.

Is he come? Then take heed each one to his thing. 200

· Et accipit clamiden ab ipso.[1]

Mak.

What! I am a yeoman — since there's need I should
    tell you — of the King,
That self-same, indeed, messenger from a great lording,
        And the like thereby.
Fie on you! Go hence
Out of my presence! 205
I must have reverence,
        And you ask "who am I!"

[1] And takes the cloak off him.

Primus Pastor.
Why dress ye it up so quaint? Mak, ye do ill!
Secundus Pastor.
But, Mak, listen, ye saint, I believe what ye will!
Tertius Pastor.
I trow the knave can feint, by the neck the devil him
    kill!   210
Mak.
I shall make complaint, and you 'll all get your fill,
      At a word from me—
And tell your doings, forsooth!
Primus Pastor.
But, Mak, is that truth?
Now take out that southern tooth   215
      And stick in a flea!

Secundus Pastor.
Mak, the devil be in your eye, verily! to a blow I 'd
    fain treat you.
Tertius Pastor.
Mak, know you not me? By God, I could beat you!

Mak.
God keep you all three! Me thought I had seen you
    — I greet you,
Ye are a fair company!
Primus Pastor.
    Oh, now you remember, you cheat, you! 220
Secundus Pastor.
    Shrew, jokes are cheap!
When thus late a man goes,
What will folk suppose?—
You 've a bad name, God knows,
      For stealing of sheep!   225

Mak.

And true as steel am I, all men know and say,
But a sickness I feel, verily, that grips me hard,
        night and day.
My belly is all awry, it is out of play —
                Tertius Pastor.
" Seldom doth the Devil lie dead by the way — "

                Mak.
                Therefore   230
Full sore am I and ill,
Though I stand stone still;
I 've not eat a needle
        This month and more.

                Primus Pastor.
How fares thy wife, by my hood, how fares she,
        ask I?   235
                Mak.
Lies asprawl, by the Rood, lo, the fire close by,
And a house-full of home-brewed she drinks full
        nigh —
Ill may speed any good thing that she will try
        Else to do! —
Eats as fast as may be,   , 240
And each year there 'll a day be
She brings forth a baby,
        And some years two.

But were I now kinder, d'ye hear, and far richer in
        purse,
Still were I eaten clear out of house and home, sirs.
And she 's a foul-favored dear, see her close, by God's
        curse!   246

No one knows or may hear, I trow, of a worse,
         Not any!
Now will ye see what I proffer? —
To give all in my coffer,   250
To-morrow next to offer
         Her head-mass penny.

Secundus Pastor.

Faith, so weary and worn is there none in this shire.
I must sleep, were I shorn of a part of my hire.

Tertius Pastor.

I'm naked, cold, and forlorn, and would fain have a
     fire.   255

Primus Pastor.

I'm clean spent, for, since morn, I've run in the
     mire.
         Watch thou, do!

Secundus Pastor.

Nay, I'll lie down hereby,
For I must sleep, truly.

Tertius Pastor.

As good a man's son was I,   260
         As any of you!
            [*They prepare to lie down.*

But, Mak, come lie here in between, if you please.

Mak.

You'll be hindered, I fear, from talking at ease,
         Indeed!
            [*He yields and lies down.*
From my top to my toe,   265
Manus tuas commendo,
Poncio Pilato,
         Christ's cross me speed!

Tunc surgit, pastoribus dormientibus, et dicit: [1]

Now 't were time a man knew, that lacks what he'd
    fain hold,
To steal privily through then into a fold,   270
And then nimbly his work do — and be not too bold,
For his bargain he'd rue, if it were told
        At the ending
Now 't were time their wrath to tell! —
But he needs good counsel   275
That fain would fare well,
        And has but little for spending.

But about you a circle as round as a moon,
            [*He draws the circle.*
Till I have done what I will, till that it be noon,
That ye lie stone still, until I have done;   280
And I shall say thereto still, a few good words soon
        Of might:
Over your heads my hand I lift.
Out go your eyes! Blind be your sight! [2]
But I must make still better shift,   285
        If it's to be right.

Lord, how hard they sleep — that may ye all hear!
I never herded sheep, but I 'll learn now, that's clear.
Though the flock be scared a heap, yet shall I slip
    near.   [*He captures a sheep.*
Hey — hitherward creep! Now that betters our cheer
        From sorrow.   291
A fat sheep, I dare say!
A good fleece, swear I may!

[1] Then he rises, when the shepherds are asleep, and says:
[2] Assonance in original.

When I can, then I 'll pay,
          But this I will borrow!   295

[*Mak goes to his house, and knocks at the door.*]
          Mak.
Ho, Gill, art thou in ? Get us a light!
          Uxor Eius.
Who makes such a din at this time of night?
I am set for to spin, I think not I might
Rise a penny to win! Curses loud on them light
          Trouble cause!   300
A busy house-wife all day
To be called thus away!
No work 's done, I say,
          Because of such small chores!

          Mak.
The door open, good Gill. See'st thou not what I
          bring ?   305
          Uxor.
Draw the latch, an thou will. Ah, come in, my sweeting!
          Mak.
Yea, thou need'st not care didst thou kill me with such
          long standing !
          Uxor.
By the naked neck still thou art likely to swing.
          Mak.
          Oh, get away!
I am worthy of my meat,   310
For at a pinch I can get
More than they that swink and sweat
          All the long day.

Thus it fell to my lot, Gill! Such luck came my way!

Uxor.

It were a foul blot to be hanged for it some day.   315

Mak.

I have often escaped, Gillot, as risky a play.

Uxor.

But " though long goes the pot to the water," men say,
                " At last
Comes it home broken."

Mak.

Well know I the token,   320
But let it never be spoken —
                But come and help fast !

I would he were slain, I would like well to eat,
This twelvemonth was I not so fain to have some
        sheep's meat.

Uxor.

Should they come ere he 's slain and hear the sheep
        bleat —   325

Mak.

Then might I be ta'en. That were a cold sweat !
                The door —
Go close it !

Uxor.

        Yes, Mak, —
For if they come at thy back —

Mak.

Then might I suffer from the whole pack   330
                The devil, and more !

Uxor.

A good trick have I spied, since thou thinkest of none,
Here shall we him hide until they be gone —
In my cradle he 'll bide — just you let me alone —
And I shall lie beside in childbed and groan.   335

Mak.
> Well said!
And I shall say that this night
A boy child saw the light.

Uxor.
> Now that day was bright
>> That saw me born and bred!   340

This is a good device and a far cast.[1]
Ever a woman's advice gives help at the last!
I care not who spies! Now go thou back fast!

Mak.
Save I come ere they rise, there 'll blow a cold blast!

[*Mak goes back to the moor, and prepares to lie down.*]
>> I will go sleep.   345
Still sleeps all this company,
And I shall slip in privily
As it had never been I
>> That carried off their sheep.

Primus Pastor.
Resurrex a mortruis! Reach me a hand!   350
Judas carnas dominus! I can hardly stand!
My foot's asleep, by Jesus, and my mouth's dry as sand.
I thought we had laid us full nigh to England!

Secundus Pastor.
>> Yea, verily!
Lord, but I have slept well.   355
As fresh as an eel,
As light do I feel,
>> As leaf on the tree.

---

[1] Far-fetched (clever) trick.

Tertius Pastor.

Ben'cite be herein! So my body is quaking,
My heart is out of my skin with the to-do it's mak-
        ing.   360
Who's making all this din, so my head's set to aching.
To the doer I'll win! Hark, you fellows, be waking!
              Four we were —
See ye aught of Mak now?

Primus Pastor.

We were up ere thou.   365

Secundus Pastor.

Man, to God I vow,   .
              Not once did he stir.

Tertius Pastor.

Methought he was lapt in a wolf's skin.

Primus Pastor.

So many are wrapped now — namely within.

Tertius Pastor.

When we had long napped, methought with a gin 370
A fat sheep he trapped, but he made no din.

Secundus Pastor.

              Be still!
Thy dream makes thee mad,
It's a nightmare you've had.

Primus Pastor.

God bring good out of bad,   375
              If it be his will!

Secundus Pastor.

Rise, Mak, for shame! Right long dost thou lie.

Mak.

Now Christ's Holy Name be with us for aye!
What's this, by Saint James, I can't move when I try.

I suppose I 'm the same. Oo-o, my neck's lain awry 380
              Enough, perdie —
Many thanks ! — since yester even.
Now, by Saint Stephen,
I was plagued by a sweven,[1]
              Knocked the heart of me.   385

I thought Gill begun to croak and travail full sad,
Well-nigh at the first cock, with a young lad
To add to our flock. Of that I am never glad,
I have " tow on my rock more than ever I had."
              Oh, my head !   390
A house full of young banes —
The devil knock out their brains !
Wo is him many gains,
              And thereto little bread.

I must go home, by your leave, to Gill, as I
       thought.   395
Prithee look in my sleeve that I steal naught.
I am loath you to grieve, or from you take aught.
              Tertius Pastor.
Go forth — ill may'st thou thrive !   [*Mak goes.*
              Now I would that we sought
              This morn,
That we had all our store.   400
              Primus Pastor.
But I will go before.
Let us meet.
              Secundus Pastor.
Where, Daw ?
              Tertius Pastor.
At the crooked thorn.

              [1] Dream.

[*They go out. Mak enters and knocks at his door.*]

Mak.

Undo the door, see who's here! How long must I
    stand?

Uxor Eius.

Who's making such gear? Now "walk in the wen-
    yand." [1]   405

Mak.

Ah, Gill, what cheer? It is I, Mak, your husband.

Uxor.

Then may we " see here the devil in a band,"
                    Sir Guile!
Lo, he comes with a note
As he were held by the throat.   410
And I cannot devote
            To my work any while.

Mak.

Will ye hear the pother she makes to get her a gloze [2]—
Naught but pleasure she takes, and curls up her toes.

Uxor.

Why, who runs, who wakes, [3] who comes, who goes, 415
Who brews, who bakes, what makes me hoarse, d'ye
    suppose!
                    And also,
It is ruth to behold,
Now in hot, now in cold,
Full woeful is the household   420
            That no woman doth know!

But what end hast thou made with the shepherds, Mak?

---

[1] See note.   [2] Excuse.
[3] Watches.

Mak.

The last word that they said when I turned my back
Was they 'd see that they had of their sheep all the
   pack.
They 'll not be pleased, I 'm afraid, when they their
   sheep lack,   425
Perdie.
But how so the game go,
They 'll suspect me, whether or no,
And raise a great bellow,
            And cry out upon me.   430

But thou must use thy sleight.

Uxor.

            Yea, I think it not ill.
I shall swaddle him aright in my cradle with skill.
Were it yet a worse plight, yet a way I 'd find still.

[*Gill meanwhile swaddles the sheep and places him in the
          cradle.*]
I will lie down forthright. Come tuck me up.

Mak.

            That I will.

Uxor.

Behind !   435
      [*Mak tucks her in at the back.*
If Coll come and his marrow,[1]
They will nip us full narrow.

Mak.

But I may cry out " Haro," [2]
      The sheep if they find.

---

[1] Company.   [2] Woe 's me ! Help !

Uxor.

Hearken close till they call — they will come anon.   440
Come and make ready all, and sing thou alone —
Sing lullaby, thou shalt, for I must groan
And cry out by the wall on Mary and John
>   Full sore.
Sing lullaby on fast,   445
When thou hear'st them at last,
And, save I play a shrewd cast,
>   Trust me no more.

[*The Shepherds enter on the moor and meet.*]

Tertius Pastor.

Ah, Coll, good morn ! Why sleepest thou not ?

Primus Pastor.

Alas, that ever I was born! We have a foul blot. 450
A fat wether have we lorn.

Tertius Pastor.

>   Marry, God forbid, say it not !

Secundus Pastor.

Who should do us that scorn ? [1] That were a foul spot.

Primus Pastor.

>   Some shrew.
I have sought with my dogs
All Horbury Shrogs,[2]   455
And of fifteen hogs [3]
>   Found I all but one ewe.

Tertius Pastor.

Now trust me, if you will, by Saint Thomas of Kent,
Either Mak or Gill their aid thereto lent !

---

[1] Evil trick.   [2] Thickets.
[3] Young sheep.

Primus Pastor.

Peace, man, be still! I saw when he went.   460
Thou dost slander him ill. Thou shouldest repent
          At once, indeed!

Secundus Pastor.

So may I thrive, perdie,
Should I die here where I be,
I would say it was he   465
          That did that same deed!

Tertius Pastor.

Go we thither, quick sped, and run on our feet,
I shall never eat bread till I know all complete!

Primus Pastor.

Nor drink in my head till with him I meet.

Secundus Pastor.

In no place will I bed until I him greet,   470
          My brother!
One vow I will plight,
Till I see him in sight,
I will ne'er sleep one night
          Where I do another!   475

[*They go to Mak's house. Mak, hearing them coming, begins to sing lullaby at the top of his voice, while Gill
groans in concert.*]

Tertius Pastor.

Hark the rów they make! List our sire there croon!

Primus Pastor.

Never heard I voice break so clear out of tune.
Call to him.

Secundus Pastor.

          Mak, wake there! Undo your door soon!

Mak.

Who is that spake as if it were noon?

Aloft? 480

Who is that, I say?

Tertius Pastor.

Good fellows, if it were day —   [*Mocking Mak.*

Mak.

As far as ye may,

Kindly, speak soft;

O'er a sick woman's head in such grievous throes! 485
I were liefer dead than she should suffer such woes.

Uxor.

Go elsewhere, well sped. Oh, how my pain grows —
Each footfall ye tread goes straight through my nose
So loud, woe 's me!

Primus Pastor.

Tell us, Mak, if ye may, 490
How fare ye, I say?

Mak.

But are ye in this town to-day —
Now how fare ye?

Ye have run in the mire and are wet still a bit,
I will make you a fire, if ye will sit. 495
A nurse I would hire — can you help me in it?
Well quit is my hire — my dream the truth hit —
In season.
I have bairns, if ye knew,
Plenty more than will do, 500
But we must drink as we brew,
And that is but reason.

I would ye would eat ere ye go. Methinks that ye sweat.

Secundus Pastor.

Nay, no help could we know in what 's drunken or eat.

Mak.

Why, sir, ails you aught but good, though?

Tertius Pastor.

                    Yea, our sheep that we got   505
Are stolen as they go; our loss is great.

Mak.

            Sirs, drink!
Had I been there,
Some one had bought it sore, I swear.

Primus Pastor.

Marry, some men trow that ye were,   510
            And that makes us think!

Secundus Pastor.

Mak, one and another trows it should be ye.

Tertius Pastor.

Either ye or your spouse, so say we.

Mak.

Now if aught suspicion throws on Gill or me,
Come and search our house, and then may ye see   515
            Who had her —
If I any sheep got,
Or cow or stot;[1]
And Gill, my wife, rose not,
            Here since we laid her.   520

As I am true and leal, to God, here I pray
That this is the first meal that I shall eat this day.

Primus Pastor.

Mak, as may I have weal, advise thee, I say —
"He learned timely to steal that could not say nay."

            [1] Bullock.

Uxor.

　　　Me, my death you 've dealt! 　　　525
Out, ye thieves, nor come again,
Ye 've come just to rob us, that 's plain.

Mak.

Hear ye not how she groans amain —
　　　Your hearts should melt!

Uxor.

From my child, thieves, begone. Go nigh him not, —
　　　there 's the door! 　　　530

Mak.

If ye knew all she 's borne, your hearts would be sore.
Ye do wrong, I you warn, thus to come in before
A woman that has borne — but I say no more.

Uxor.

　　　Oh, my middle — I die!
I vow to God so mild, 　　　535
If ever I you beguiled,
That I will eat this child
　　　That doth in this cradle lie!

Mak.

Peace, woman, by God's pain, and cry not so.
Thou dost hurt thy brain and fill me with woe. 　　　540

Secundus Pastor.

I trow our sheep is slain. What find ye two, though?
Our work 's all in vain. We may as well go.
　　　Save clothes and such matters
I can find no flesh
Hard or nesh, 　　　545
Salt nor fresh,
　　　Except two empty platters.

Of any " cattle " [1] but this, tame or wild, that we see,
None, as may I have bliss, smelled as loud as he.

Uxor.

No, so God joy and bliss of my child may give me!

Primus Pastor.

We have aimed amiss; deceived, I trow, were we. 551

Secundus Pastor.

  Sir, wholly each, one.
Sir, Our Lady him save!
Is your child a knave?

Mak.

Any lord might him have,   555
  This child, for his son.

When he wakes, so he grips, it 's a pleasure to see.

Tertius Pastor.

Good luck to his hips,[2] and blessing, say we!
But who were his gossips,[3] now tell who they be?

Mak.

Blest be their lips —   [*Hesitates, at a loss.*

Primus Pastor.

  Hark a lie now, trust me!   [*Aside.* 560

Mak.

  So may God them thank,
Parkin and Gibbon Waller, I say,
And gentle John Horn, in good fey — [4]
He made all the fun and play —
  With the great shank.[5]   565

Secundus Pastor.

Mak, friends will we be, for we are at one.

---

[1] See note.   [2] See note.
[3] Sponsors.   [4] Faith.
[5] Long legs.

Mak.

We! — nay, count not on me, for amends get I none.
Farewell, all three! Glad 't will be when ye 're gone!

                            [*The Shepherds go.*

Tertius Pastor.

" Fair words there may be, but love there is none
              This year."   570

Primus Pastor.

Gave ye the child anything?

Secundus Pastor.

I trow, not one farthing.

Tertius Pastor.

Fast back I will fling.
          Await ye me here.

[*Daw goes back. The other Shepherds turn and follow
him slowly, entering while he is talking with Mak.*]

[*Tertius Pastor.*]

Mak, I trust thou 'lt not grieve, if I go to thy
      child.   575

Mak.

Nay, great hurt I receive, — thou hast acted full wild.

Tertius Pastor.

Thy bairn 't will not grieve, little day-star so mild.
Mak, by your leave, let me give your child
          But six-pence.

[*Daw goes to cradle, and starts to draw away the
covering.*]

Mak.

Nay, stop it — he sleeps!   580

Tertius Pastor.

Methinks he peeps —

Mak.

When he wakens, he weeps ;
            I pray you go hence !
                        [*The other Shepherds return.*

Tertius Pastor.

Give me leave him to kiss, and lift up the clout.[1]
What the devil is this ? — he has a long snout !   585
                        Primus Pastor.
He 's birth-marked amiss. We waste time hereabout.
                        Secundus Pastor.
" A weft that ill-spun is comes ever foul out."
                                    [*He sees the sheep.*
            Aye — so !
He is like to our sheep !
                        Tertius Pastor.
Ho, Gib, may I peep ?   590
                        Primus Pastor.
I trow " Nature will creep
            Where it may not go."

Secundus Pastor.

This was a quaint gaud [2] and a far cast.
It was a high fraud.
                        Tertius Pastor.
            Yea, sirs, that was 't.
Let 's burn this bawd, and bind her fast.   595
" A false scold," by the Lord, " will hang at the last ! "
            So shalt thou !
Will ye see how they swaddle
His four feet in the middle !   ·
Saw I never in the cradle   600
            A horned lad ere now !

---

[1] Cloth.   [2] Shrewd trick.

Mak.

Peace, I say! Tell ye what, this to-do ye can spare!

　　　　　　　　　　　　[Pretending anger.

It was I him begot and yon woman him bare.

Primus Pastor.

What the devil for name has he got? Mak?—
Lo, God, Mak's heir!

Secundus Pastor.

Come, joke with him not. Now, may God give him care,
　　　　　I say!　　　　　　　　606

Uxor.

A pretty child is he
As sits on a woman's knee,
A dilly-down,[1] perdie,
　　　　To make a man gay.　　　610

Tertius Pastor.

I know him by the ear-mark — that is a good token.

Mak.

I tell you, sirs, hark, his nose was broken —
Then there told me a clerk he 'd been mis-spoken.[2]

Primus Pastor.

Ye deal falsely and dark; I would fain be wroken.[3]
　　　　Get a weapon, — go!　　　615

Uxor.

He was taken by an elf,
I saw it myself.
When the clock struck twelve,
　　　　Was he mis-shapen so.

Secundus Pastor.

Ye two are at one, that 's plain, in all ye 've done and
　　　said.　　　　　　　620

[1] Darling.　　　[2] Bewitched.　　　[3] Revenged.

Primus Pastor.

Since their theft they maintain, let us leave them
    dead!

Mak.

If I trespass again, strike off my head!
At your will I remain.

             Tertius Pastor.

             Sirs, take my counsel instead.

For this trespass

We 'll neither curse nor wrangle in spite,   625
Chide nor fight,
But have done forthright,
           And toss him in canvas.

[*They toss Mak in one of Gill's canvas sheets till they are
tired. He disappears groaning into his house. The
Shepherds pass over to the moor on the other side of
the stage.*]

             Primus Pastor.

Lord, lo! but I am sore, like to burst, in back and
    breast.
In faith, I may no more, therefore will I rest.   630

             Secundus Pastor.

Like a sheep of seven score he weighed in my fist.
To sleep anywhere, therefore seemeth now best.

             Tertius Pastor.

             Now I you pray,
On this green let us lie.

             Primus Pastor.

O'er those thieves yet chafe I.   635

             Tertius Pastor.

Let your anger go by, —
             Come do as I say.

[*As they are about to lie down the Angel appears.*]

Angelus cantat " Gloria in excelsis." Postea dicat : [1]
Angelus.

Rise, herdsmen gentle, attend ye, for now is he born
From the fiend that shall rend what Adam had lorn,
That warlock to shend,[2] this night is he born,   640
God is made your friend now on this morn.
     Lo! thus doth he command —
Go to Bethlehem, see
Where he lieth so free,[3]
In a manger full lowly   645
     'Twixt where twain beasts stand.
                [*The Angel goes.*

Primus Pastor.

This was a fine voice, even as ever I heard.
It is a marvel, by St. Stephen, thus with dread to be
    stirred.

Secundus Pastor.

'T was of God's Son from heaven he these tidings
    averred.
All the wood with a levin,[4] methought at his word 650
     Shone fair.

Tertius Pastor.

Of a Child did he tell,
In Bethlehem, mark ye well.

Primus Pastor.

That this star yonder doth spell —
     Let us seek him there.   655

Secundus Pastor.

Say, what was his song — how it went, did ye hear?
Three breves to a long —

---

[1] The Angel sings the " Gloria in Excelsis." Then let him say:
[2] Spoil, overthrow.   [3] Noble.   [4] Lightning.

Tertius Pastor.

Marry, yes, to my ear
There was no crotchet wrong, naught it lacked and full
　　clear!

Primus Pastor.

To sing it here, us among, as he nicked it, full near,
　　　　　I know how —　　　　　　　.　　　　660

Secundus Pastor.

Let's see how you croon!
Can you bark at the moon?

Tertius Pastor.

Hold your tongues, have done!
　　　　　Hark after me now!　　　　*[They sing.*

Secundus Pastor.

To Bethlehem he bade that we should go.　　　665
I am sore adrad [1] that we tarry too slow.

Tertius Pastor.

Be merry, and not sad — our song's of mirth not of
　　woe, ·
To be forever glad as our meed may we know,
　　　　　Without noise.

Primus Pastor.

Hie we thither, then, speedily,　　　　　670
Though we be wet and weary,
To that Child and that Lady! —
　　　　　We must not lose those joys!

Secundus Pastor.

We find by the prophecy — let be your din! —
David　and　Isaiah,　and　more　that　I　mind　me
　　　therein,　　　　　　　　　　　675

[1] Adread.

They prophesied by clergy, that in a virgin,
Should he alight and lie, to assuage our sin,
        And slake it,
Our nature, from woe,
For it was Isaiah said so,   680
" *Ecce virgo*
     Concipiet " a child that is naked.

Tertius Pastor.

Full glad may we be and await that day
That lovesome one to see, that all mights doth sway.
Lord, well it were with me, now and for aye,   685
Might I kneel on my knee some word for to say
        To that child.
But the angel said
In a crib was he laid,
He was poorly arrayed,   690
       Both gracious and mild.

Primus Pastor.

Patriarchs that have been and prophets beforne,[1]
They desired to have seen this child that is born.
They are gone full clean, — that have they lorn.
We shall see him, I ween, ere it be morn,   695
       For token.
When I see him and feel,
I shall know full well,
It is true as steel,
       What prophets have spoken,   700

To so poor as we are that he would appear,
First find and declare by his messenger.

[1] Before.

Secundus Pastor.

Go we now, let us fare, the place is us near.

Tertius Pastor.

I am ready and eager to be there; let us together with
    cheer

             To that bright one go.   705

Lord, if thy will it be,

Untaught are we all three,

Some kind of joy grant us, that we

         Thy creatures, comfort may know!

[*They enter the stable and adore the infant Saviour.*]

Primus Pastor.

Hail, thou comely and clean one! Hail, young Child! 710

Hail, Maker, as I mean, from a maiden so mild!

Thou hast harried, I ween, the warlock so wild, —

The false beguiler with his teen now goes beguiled.

        Lo, he merries,

Lo, he laughs, my sweeting!   715

A happy meeting!

Here's my promised greeting, —

      Have a bob of cherries!

Secundus Pastor.

Hail, sovereign Saviour, for thou hast us sought!

Hail, noble nursling and flower, that all things hast
    wrought!   720

Hail, thou, full of gracious power, that made all from
    nought!

Hail, I kneel and I cower! A bird have I brought

       To my bairn from far.

Hail, little tiny mop![1]

         [1] See note.

Of our creed thou art the crop,[1]   725
I fain would drink in thy cup,
        Little day-star!

Tertius Pastor.

Hail, darling dear one, full of Godhead indeed!
I pray thee be near, when I have need.
Hail, sweet is thy cheer! My heart would bleed   730
To see thee sit here in so poor a weed,[2]
        With no pennies.
Hail, put forth thy dall,[3]
I bring thee but a ball.
Keep it, and play with it withal,   735
        And go to the tennis.

Maria.

The Father of Heaven this night, God omnipotent,
That setteth all things aright, his Son hath he sent.
My name he named and did light on me ere that he
        went.
I conceived him forthright through his might as he .
        meant,   740
        And now he is born.
May he keep you from woe!
I shall pray him do so.
Tell it, forth as ye go,
        And remember this morn.   745

Primus Pastor.

Farewell, Lady, so fair to behold
With thy child on thy knee!

---

[1] Head, topmost part.   [2] Dress, covering.
[3] Fist.

Secundus Pastor.

                       But he lies full cold!

Lord, 't is well with me! Now we go, behold!

Tertius Pastor.

Forsooth, already it seems to be told

                Full oft!   750

Primus Pastor.

What grace we have found!

Secundus Pastor.

Now are we won safe and sound.

Tertius Pastor.

Come forth, to sing are we bound.

               Make it ring then aloft!

                          [*They depart singing.*

           Explicit pagina Pastorum.[1]

     [1] Here endeth the play of the Shepherds.

EVERYMAN

[THE text of *Everyman* is preserved in four early editions, two of which were printed by Pynson (1493–1530), and two by Skot (1521–1537). Their precise date is not known (see Logeman). The play was included in Hawkins's *Origin of the English Drama*, 1773, in Dodsley's *Select Collection of Old English Plays*, 1874 (and 1902), and has since been reprinted frequently in scholarly and popular editions as follows: Shakespeare Society, *Papers*, vol. iii, 1849; by Pollard (in part), *English Miracle Plays, Moralities, and Interludes* (3d edition), 1898; H. Logeman, *Elckerlijk*, 1892 (the Dutch version with a reprint of one of Skot's editions, collated with his other edition and those of Pynson), also, 1902 (with an introduction by F. Sidgwick); S. M. 1903 (with reproductions of photographs of Mr. Greet's production); W. W. Greg, 1904 (edition of Skot at Britwell Court); also 1909 (edition of Skot in possession of A. H. Huth), with musical setting by H. Walford Davies, 1904; J. S. Farmer, *Six Anonymous Plays*, 1905, also in the *Museum Dramatists*, 1906 (with critical apparatus), illustrated by Ambrose Dudley, 1906; *Broadway Booklets*, 1906; "*Everyman*" with other *Interludes*, "Everyman's Library" (no date; individual editor not indicated, under general editorship of Ernest Rhys), etc. The editions of value are those of Pollard (though parts only are given), Logeman, and Greg.

The opinion has been commonly accepted that the English version of the play was a translation from the Dutch version *Elckerlyc* (*Elckerlijk*) ascribed to Dorlandus, and this view has been ably supported by Logeman (editions as above, and *Elckerlyk-Everyman: De vraag naar de Prioriteit opnieuw onderzocht*, 1902). The chief support of this view is the fact that the Dutch version was printed before the English. It is safer to consider the question still open. Either may be the earlier, and both may go back to an earlier version now lost. See also Schelling, vol. ii, 450.

For comment upon the play, see the *Introduction.*]

Here beginneth a treatise how the High Father of Heaven sendeth Death to summon every creature to come and give an account of their lives in this world, and is in manner of a moral play.

[*The Messenger enters.*

Messenger.

I pray you all give your audience,
And hear this matter with reverence,
   In form a <u>moral play.</u>
The Summoning of Everyman it is called so,
That of our lives and ending maketh show   5
   How transitory we be every day.
This matter is wondrous precious,
But the meaning of it is more gracious
   And sweet to bear away.
The story saith: Man, in the beginning   10
Watch well, and take good heed of the ending,
   Be you never so gay!
Ye think sin in the beginning full sweet,
Which, in the end, causeth the soul to weep,
   When the body lieth in clay.   15

Here shall you see how Fellowship and Jollity,
Both Strength, Pleasure, and Beauty,
   Will fade from thee as flower in May,
For ye shall hear how our Heaven's King
Calleth Everyman to a general reckoning.   20
   Give audience and hear what he doth say.
                         [*The Messenger goes.*

          God speaketh:
I perceive, here in my majesty,
   How that all creatures be to me unkind,
Living, without fear, in worldly prosperity.
   In spiritual vision the people be so blind,   · 25
Drowned in sin, they know me not for their God;
   In worldly riches is all their mind.
They fear not my righteousness, the sharp rod.
   My law that I disclosed, when I for them died,
They clean forget, and shedding of my blood red.   30
   I hung between two it cannot be denied,
To get them life I suffered to be dead,
I healed their feet, with thorns was hurt my head.
   I could do no more than I did truly,
   And now I see the people do clean forsake me;   35
They use the seven deadly sins damnable
   In such wise that pride, covetousness, wrath, and
      lechery,
Now in this world be made commendable,
   And thus they leave of angels the heavenly company.
Every man liveth so after his own pleasure,   40
And yet of their lives they be nothing sure.
The more I them forbear, I see
The worse from year to year they be;
All that live grow more evil apace;
Therefore I will, in briefest space,   45

From every man in person have a reckoning shown.
For, if I leave the people thus alone
In their way of life and wicked passions to be,
They will become much worse than beasts, verily.
Now for envy would one eat up another, and tarry not,
Charity is by all clean forgot.   51
I hoped well that every man
In my glory should make his mansion,
And thereto I made them all elect,
But now I see, like traitors abject,   55
They thank me not for the pleasure that I for them
     ·   meant,
Nor yet for their being that I them have lent.
I proffered the people great multitude of mercy,
And few there be that ask it heartily.
They be so cumbered with worldly riches, thereto   60
I must needs upon them justice do, —
On every man living without fear.
Where art thou, Death, thou mighty messenger?
                               [*Death enters.*

Death.

Almighty God, I am here at your will,
Your commandment to fulfil.   65

God.

Go thou to Everyman,
And show him in my name
A pilgrimage he must on him take,
Which he in no wise may escape,
And that he bring with him a sure reckoning   70
Without delay or any tarrying.

Death.

Lord, I will in the world go run over all,
And cruelly search out both great and small.

Every man will I beset that liveth beastly
Out of God's law, and doth not dread folly.   75
He that loveth riches I will strike with my dart
His sight to blind and him from heaven to part —
Except if Alms be his good friend —
In hell for to dwell, world without end.
Lo, yonder I see Everyman walking.   80
Full little he thinketh on my coming!
His mind is on fleshly lusts and his treasure,
And great pain it shall cause him to endure
Before the Lord, of Heaven the King.
Everyman, stand still! Whither art thou going   85
Thus gayly? Hast thou thy Maker forgot?

                                [*Everyman enters.*

Everyman.

  Why askest thou?
Wouldest thou know? For what?

            Death.

  Yea, sir, I will show you now.
In great haste I am sent to thee   90
From God, out of his majesty.

          Everyman.

What, sent to me!

           Death.

Yea, certainly.
Though thou hast forgot him here,
He thinketh on thee in the heavenly sphere,   95
As, ere we part, thou shalt know.

          Everyman.

What desireth God of me?

           Death.

That shall I show thee.
A reckoning he will needs have
  Without any longer respite.   100

Everyman.

To give a reckoning longer leisure I crave.
  This blind matter troubleth my wit.

Death.

Upon thee thou must take a long journey,
  Therefore, do thou thine accounting-book with thee
    bring.
For turn again thou canst not by no way,   105
  And look thou be sure in thy reckoning,
For before God thou shalt answer, and show true
Thy many bad deeds and good but a few,
How thou hast spent thy life and in what wise
Before the Chief Lord of Paradise.   110
Get thee prepared that we may be upon that journey,
For well thou knowest thou shalt make none for thee
      attorney.

Everyman.

Full unready I am such reckoning to give.
I know thee not. What messenger art thou?

Death.

I am Death that no man fear,   115
For every man I arrest and no man spare,
For it is God's commandment
That all to me should be obedient.

Everyman.

O Death, thou comest when I had thee least in mind!
  In thy power it lieth to save me yet; —   120
Thereto of my goods will I give thee, if thou wilt be
    kind, —
  Yea, a thousand pounds shalt thou get! —
And defer this matter till another day.

Death.

Everyman, it may not be in any way.
I set no store by gold, silver, riches, or such gear, 125

Nor by pope, emperor, king, prince, or peer.
For, if I would receive gifts great,
All the world I might get,
But my custom is clean the contrary way.
I give thee no respite. Come hence, nor delay!   130

Everyman.

Alas, shall I have no longer respite!
  I may say Death giveth no warning!
To think on thee, it maketh my heart sick,
  For all unready is my book of reckoning.
  But if I might have twelve years of waiting,   135
My accounting-book I would make so clear
That my reckoning I should not need to fear.
Wherefore, Death, I pray thee, for God's mercy,
Spare me till I be provided with a remedy!

Death.

It availeth thee not to cry, weep, and pray,   140
But haste thee lightly, that thou mayest be on thy
      journey,
And make proof of thy friends, if thou can,
For, know thou well, time waiteth for no man,
And in the world each living creature
Because of Adam's sin must die by nature.   145

Everyman.

Death, if I should this pilgrimage take,
And my reckoning duly make,
Show me, for Saint Charity,
Should I not come again shortly?

Death.

No, Everyman, if once thou art there,   150
Thou mayest nevermore come here,
Trust me, verily.

Everyman.

O gracious God, in the high seat celestial,
Have mercy on me in this utmost need!
Shall I no company have from this vale terrestrial 155
Of mine acquaintance that way me to lead?

Death.

Yea, if any be so hardy
As to go with thee and bear thee company.
Haste thee that thou mayest be gone to God's magnifi-
cence,
Thy reckoning to give before his presence.   160
What, thinkest thou thy life is given thee,
And thy worldly goods also?

Everyman.

I had thought so, verily.

Death.

Nay, nay, it was but lent to thee,
For, as soon as thou dost go,   165
Another a while shall have it and then even so,
Go therefore as thou hast done.
Everyman, thou art mad! Thou hast thy wits five,
And here on earth will not amend thy life,
For suddenly I do come!   170

Everyman.

O wretched caitiff, whither shall I flee
That I may escape this endless sorrow!
Nay, gentle Death, spare me until to-morrow
That I may amend me
With good avisement!   175

Death.

Nay, thereto I will not consent,
Nor no man respite, if I might,
But to the heart suddenly I shall smite

Without any " advisement."
And now out of thy sight I will me hie,   180
See that thou make thee ready speedily,
For thou mayest say this is the day
Wherefrom no man living may escape away.

Everyman.

Alas, I may well weep with sighs deep!
    Now have I no manner of company   185
To help me on my journey and me to keep,
    And also my writing is all unready.
What can I do that may excuse me!
    I would to God I had never been begot!
To my soul a full great profit it would be,   190
    For now I fear pains huge and great, God wot!
The time passeth — help, Lord, that all things
            wrought!
For, though I mourn, yet it availeth naught.
The day passeth and is almost through,
I wot not well of aught that I may do.   195
To whom were it best that I my plaint should make?
What if to Fellowship I thereof spake,
And what this sudden chance should mean disclosed?
For surely in him is all my trust reposed —
We have in the world so many a day   200
Been good friends in sport and play.
I see him yonder certainly —
I trust that he will bear me company;
Therefore to him will I speak to ease my sorrow.
Well met, good Fellowship, and a good morrow!   205

                    [*Enter Fellowship*

Fellowship speaketh :

I wish thee good morrow, Everyman, by this day!
    Sir, why lookest thou so piteously?

If anything be amiss, prithee to me it say
  That I may help in remedy.

Everyman.

Yea, good Fellowship, yea,   210
  I am in great jeopardy!

Fellowship.

My true friend, show to me your mind.
I will not forsake thee to my live's end,
In the way of good company.

Everyman.

That was well spoken and lovingly.   215

Fellowship.

Sir, I must needs know your heaviness.
I have pity to see you in any distress.
If any have wronged you, revenged ye shall be,
Though I upon the ground be slain for thee,
Even should I know before that I should die.   220

Everyman.

Verily, Fellowship, gramercy!

Fellowship.

Tush! By thy thanks I set not a straw.
Show me your grief and say no more.

Everyman.

If I my heart should to you unfold,
  And you then were to turn your heart from me, 225
And no comfort would give when I had told,
  Then should I ten times sorrier be.

Fellowship.

Sir, I say as I will do indeed!

Everyman.

Then you be a good friend at need.
I have found you true heretofore.   230

Fellowship.

And so ye shall evermore,
For, in faith, if thou goest to hell,
 I will not forsake thee by the way.

Everyman.

Ye speak like a good friend — I believe you well.
 I shall deserve it, if so I may!   235

Fellowship.

I speak of no deserving, by this day,
For he that will say, and nothing do,
Is not worthy with good company to go.
Therefore show me the grief of your mind,
As to your friend most loving and kind.   240

Everyman.

I shall show you how it is:
 Commanded I am to go a journey,
A long way hard and dangerous,
 And give a strict account without delay
 Before the High Judge, Adonai.   245
Wherefore, I pray you, bear me company,
As ye have promised, on this journey.

Fellowship.

That is matter, indeed! Promise is duty —
But if I should take such a voyage on me,
I know well it should be to my pain;   25(
Afeard also it maketh me, for certain.
But let us take counsel here as well as we can,
For your words would dismay a strong man.

Everyman.

Why, if I had need, ye said
Ye would never forsake me, quick nor dead,   255
Though it were to hell truly!

Fellowship.

So I said certainly,
But such pleasant things be set aside, the truth to
    say;
And also, if we took such a journey,
When should we come again?   260

Everyman.

Nay, never again till the day of doom.

Fellowship.

In faith, then, will I not come there.
  Who hath you these tidings brought?

Everyman.

Indeed, Death was with me here.

Fellowship.

  Now, by God that all hath bought,   265
If Death were the messenger,
For no man living here below
I will not that loathly journey go —
Not for the father that begat me!

Everyman.

Ye promised otherwise, pardy!   270

Fellowship.

I know well I do say so, truly,
  And still, if thou wilt eat and drink and make good
    cheer,
Or haunt of women the merry company,
  I would not forsake you while the day is clear,
Trust me, verily.   275

Everyman.

Yea, thereto ye would be ready!
  To go to mirth, solace, and play,
Your mind would sooner persuaded be
  Than to bear me company on my long journey.

Fellowship.

Now, in good sooth, I have no will that way — 280
But if thou would'st murder, or any man kill,
In that I will help thee with a good will.

Everyman.

Oh, that is simple advice, indeed !
  Gentle Fellowship, help me in my necessity !
We have loved long, and now I am in need ! 285
  And now, gentle Fellowship, remember me !

Fellowship.

Whether ye have loved me or no,
By Saint John, I will not with thee go !

Everyman.

Yea, I pray thee, take this task on thee and do so
    much for me,
As to bring me forward on my way for Saint
    Charity, 290
And comfort me till I come without the town.

Fellowship.

Nay, if thou wouldest give me a new gown,
I will not a foot with thee go.
But, if thou hadst tarried, I would not have left
    thee so.
And so now, God speed thee on thy journey, 295
For from thee I will depart as fast as I may !

Everyman.

Whither away, Fellowship ? Will you forsake me ?

Fellowship.

Yea, by my faith ! I pray God take thee.

Everyman.

Farewell, good Fellowship, — for thee my heart is
    sore.
Adieu forever, I shall see thee no more ! 300

Fellowship.

In faith, Everyman, farewell now at the ending.
For you I will remember that parting is grieving.

[*Fellowship goes.*

Everyman.

Alack! Shall we thus part indeed?
   Ah, Lady, help! Lo, vouchsafing no more comfort,
Fellowship thus forsaketh me in my utmost need. 305
   For help in this world whither shall I resort?
Fellowship heretofore with me would merry make,
And now little heed of my sorrow doth he take.
It is said in prosperity men friends may find
Which in adversity be full unkind.   31*J*
Now whither for succor shall I flee,
Since that Fellowship hath forsaken me?
To my kinsmen will I truly,
Praying them to help me in my necessity.
I believe that they will do so   315
For "Nature will creep where it may not go."

[*Kindred and Cousin enter.*

I will go try, for yonder I see them go.
Where be ye now, my friends and kinsmen, lo?

Kindred.

Here we be now at your commandment.
Cousin, I pray you show us your intent   320
In any wise and do not spare.

Cousin.

Yea, Everyman, and to us declare
If ye be disposed to go any whither,
For, wit you well, we will live and die together!

Kindred.

In wealth and woe we will with you hold,   325
For "with his own kin a man may be bold."

Everyman.

Gramercy, my friends and kinsmen kind !
Now shall I show you the grief of my mind.
I was commanded by a messenger
That is a High King's chief officer.   330
He bade me go a pilgrimage to my pain,
And I know well I shall never come again ;
And I must give a reckoning strait,[1]
For I have a great enemy that lieth for me in wait,
Who intendeth me to hinder.   335

Kindred.

What account is that which you must render ? —
That would I know.

Everyman.

Of all my works I must show
How I have lived and my days have spent,
    Also of evil deeds to which I have been used   340
In my time, since life was to me lent,
    And of all virtues that I have refused.
Therefore, I pray you, go thither with me
To help to make my account, for Saint Charity !

Cousin.

What, to go thither ? Is that the matter ?   345
Nay, Everyman, I had liefer fast on bread and water
All this five year and more !

Everyman.

Alas, that ever my mother me bore !
For now shall I never merry be,
If that you forsake me !   350

Kindred.

Ah, sir, come ! Ye be a merry man !
    Pluck up heart and make no moan.

---

[1] Strict.

But one thing I warn you, by Saint Anne,
  As for me, ye shall go alone!
Everyman.

My cousin, will you not with me go?   355
Cousin.

No, by our Lady! I have the cramp in my toe.
Trust not to me, for, so God me speed,
I will deceive you in your utmost need.
Kindred.

It availeth not us' to coax and court.
  Ye shall have my maid, with all my heart.   360
She loveth to go to feasts, there to make foolish sport
  And to dance, and in antics to take part.
To help you on that journey I will give her leave will-
    ingly,
If so be that you and she may agree.
Everyman.

Now show me the very truth within your mind — 365
Will you go with me or abide behind?
Kindred.

Abide behind? Yea, that I will, if I may —
Therefore farewell till another day!
Everyman.

How shall I be merry or glad? —
  For fair promises men to me make,   370
  But, when I have most need, they me forsake!
I am deceived — that maketh me sad!
Cousin.

Cousin Everyman, farewell now, lo!
For, verily, I will not with thee go.
Also of mine own an unready reckoning,   375
I have to give account of, therefore I make tarrying.
Now God keep thee, for now I go!
[*Kindred and Cousin go.*

Everyman.

Ah, Jesus, is all to this come so?
Lo, " fair words make fools fain,"
They promise, and from deeds refrain.   380
My kinsmen promised me faithfully
For to abide by me stedfastly,
And now fast away do they flee.
Even so Fellowship promised me.
What friend were it best for me to provide?   385
I am losing my time longer here to abide.
Yet still in my mind a thing there is,
All my life I have loved riches.
If that my Goods now help me might,
He would make my heart full light.   390
To him will I speak in my sorrow this day.
My Goods and Riches, where art thou, pray?

    [*Goods is disclosed hemmed in by chests and bags.*

Goods.

Who calleth me? Everyman? Why this haste thou
    hast?
  I lie here in corners trussed and piled so high,
And in chests I am locked so fast,   395
  Also sacked in bags, thou mayest see with thine
    eye,
I cannot stir; in packs, full low I lie.
What ye would have, lightly to me say.

Everyman.

Come hither, Goods, with all the haste thou may,
For counsel straightway I must ask of thee.   400

Goods.

Sir, if ye in this world have sorrow or adversity,
That can I help you to remedy shortly.

Everyman.

It is another disease that grieveth me;
In 'this world it is not, I tell thee so,
I am sent for another way to go,   405
To give a strict account general
Before the highest Jupiter of all.
And all my life I have had joy and pleasure in thee,
Therefore I pray thee go with me,
For, peradventure, thou mayest before God Almighty
      on high   410
My reckoning help to clean and purify,
For one may hear ever and anon
That " money maketh all right that is wrong."

Goods.

Nay, Everyman, I sing another song —
I follow no man on such voyages,   415
For, if I went with thee,
Thou shouldest fare much the worse for me,
For, because on me thou didst set thy mind,
Thy reckoning I have made blotted and blind,
So that thine account thou canst not make truly — 420
And that hast thou for the love of me.

Everyman.

That would be to me grief full sore and sorrowing,
When I should come that fearful answering.
Up, let us go thither together !

Goods.

Nay, not so ! I am too brittle, I may not endure, 425
I will follow no man one foot, be ye sure.

Everyman.

Alas ! I have thee loved, and had great pleasure
All the days of my life in goods and treasure.

Goods.

That is to thy damnation, I tell thee a true thing,
For love of me is to the love everlasting contrary. 430
But if thou hadst the while loved me moderately,
In such wise as to give the poor a part of me, ↲
Then would'st thou not in this dolor be,
Nor in this great sorrow and care.

Everyman.

Lo, now was I deceived ere I was ware,   435
And all I may blame to misspending of time.

Goods.

What, thinkest thou I am thine ?

Everyman.

I had thought so.

Goods.

Nay, Everyman, I say no.
Just for a while I was lent to thee,   440
A season thou hast had me in prosperity.
My nature it is man's soul to kill,
If I save one, a thousand I do spill.
Thinkest thou that I will follow thee?
Nay, from this world not, verily !   445

Everyman.

I had thought otherwise.

Goods.

So it is to thy soul Goods is a thief,
For when thou art dead I straightway devise
Another to deceive in the same wise
As I have done thee, and all to his soul's grief. 450

Everyman.

O false Goods, cursed may thou be !
Thou traitor to God that hast deceived me,
And caught me in thy snare.

Goods.

Marry, thou broughtest thyself to this care, —
Whereof I am glad!   455
I must needs laugh, I cannot be sad!

Everyman.

Ah, Goods, thou hast had long my hearty love.
I gave thee that which should be the Lord's above.
But wilt thou not go with me, indeed? —
    I pray thee truth to say!   460

Goods.

No, so God me speed!
    Therefore farewell, and have good-day.

                     [Goods is hidden from view.

Everyman.

Oh, to whom shall I make my moan
    For to go with me on that heavy journey!
First Fellowship, so he said, would have with me
        gone,   465
    His words were very pleasant and gay,
But afterwards he left me alone;
Then spake I to my kinsmen, all in despair,
And they also gave me words fair,
They lacked not fair speeches to spend,   470
But all forsook me in the end;
Then went I to my Goods that I loved best,
In hope to have comfort, but there had I least,
For my Goods sharply did me tell
That he bringeth many into hell.   475
Then of myself I was ashamed,
And so I am worthy to be blamed.
Thus may I well myself hate.
Of whom shall I now counsel take?
I think that I shall never speed   480
Till I go to my Good Deeds.

But, alas! she is so weak,
That she can neither move nor speak.
Yet will I venture on her now.   484
My Good Deeds, where be you?   [*Good Deeds is shown.*

Good Deeds.

Here I lie, cold in the ground.
Thy sins surely have me bound
That I cannot stir.

Everyman.

O Good Deeds, I stand in fear!
I must pray you for counsel,   490
For help now would come right well!

Good Deeds.

Everyman, I have understanding
    That ye be summoned your account to make
Before Messias, of Jerusalem King.
    If you do my counsel, that journey with you will I
        take.   495

Everyman.

    For that I come to you my moan to make.
I pray you that ye will go with me.

Good Deeds.

I would full fain, but I cannot stand, verily.

Everyman.

Why, is there something amiss that did you befall?

Good Deeds.

Yea, Sir, I may thank you for all.   500
If in every wise ye had encouraged me,
Your book of account full ready would be.
Behold the books of your works and your deeds thereby.
Ah, see, how under foot they lie
    Unto your soul's deep heaviness.   505

Everyman.

Our Lord Jesus his help vouchsafe to me,
For one letter here I cannot see.

Good Deeds.

There is a blind reckoning in time of distress!

Everyman.

Good Deeds, I pray you help me in this need,
Or else I am forever damned indeed.   510
Therefore help me to make reckoning
Before him, that Redeemer is of everything,
That is, and was, and shall ever be, King of All.

Good Deeds.

Everyman, I am sorry for your fall,
And fain would I help you, if I were able.   515

Everyman.

Good Deeds, your counsel, I pray you, give me.

Good Deeds.

That will I do, verily.
Though on my feet I may not go,
I have a sister that shall with you be, also,
Called Knowledge, who shall with you abide, 520
To help you to make that dire reckoning. .

         [Knowledge enters.

Knowledge.

Everyman, I will go with thee and be thy guide,
In thy utmost need to go by thy side.

Everyman.

In good condition I am now in every thing,
And am wholly content with this good thing, 525
Thanks be to God, my creator!

Good Deeds.

And when he hath brought thee there,
Where thou shalt heal thee of thy smart,

Then go with thy reckoning and thy good deeds to-
    gether,
  For to make thee joyful at heart   530
Before the Holy Trinity.

Everyman.

My Good Deeds, gramercy!
I am well content, certainly,
With your words sweet.

Knowledge.

Now go we together lovingly   535
To Confession, that cleansing river fair.

Everyman.

For joy I weep — I would we were there!
But, I pray you, give me cognition,
Where dwelleth that holy man, Confession?

Knowledge.

In the House of Salvation.   540
We shall find him in that place,
That shall us comfort by God's grace.

         [*Confession enters.*

Lo, this is Confession. Kneel down, and ask mercy,
For he is in good favor with God Almighty.

Everyman.

O glorious fountain that all uncleanness doth clarify, 545
Wash from me the spots of vice unclean,
That on me no sin be seen!
I come with Knowledge for my redemption,
Redeemed with heartfelt and full contrition,
For I am commanded a pilgrimage to take,   550
And great accounts before God to make.
Now I pray you, Shrift, Mother of Salvation,
Help my good deeds because of my piteous exclamation!

Confession.

I know your sorrow well, Everyman,
  Because with Knowledge ye come to me.   555
I will you comfort as well as I can,
  And a precious stone will I give thee,
  Called penance, voice-voider of adversity.
  Therewith shall your body chastened be
Through abstinence and perseverance in God's ser-
        vice.   560
Here shall you receive that scourge of me
That is penance stronge, that ye must endure,
To remember thy Saviour was scourged for thee
With sharp scourges, and suffered it patiently —
So must thou ere thou escape from that painful pil-
        grimage.   565
Knowledge, do thou sustain him on this voyage,
And by that time Good Deeds will be with thee.
But in any case be sure of mercy,
For your time draweth on fast, if ye will saved be.
Ask God mercy, and he will grant it truly.   570
When with the scourge of penance man doth him bind,
The oil of forgiveness then shall he find.

                                 [*Confession goes.*
                Everyman.

Thanked be God for his gracious work,
  For now will I my penance begin.
This hath rejoiced and lightened my heart,   575
  Though the knots be painful and hard within.

                Knowledge.

Everyman, see that ye your penance fulfil,
  Whatever the pains ye abide full dear,
And Knowledge shall give you counsel at will,
  How your account ye shall make full clear.   580

Everyman.

O eternal God, O heavenly being,
O way of righteousness, O goodly vision,
Which descended down into a virgin pure
Because he would for every man redeem
  That which Adam forfeited by his disobedience —
O blessed God, elect and exalted in thy divinity, 586
  Forgive thou my grievous offence!
  Here I cry thee mercy in this presence.

O spiritual treasure, O ransomer and redeemer,
Of all the world the hope and the governor, 590
Mirror of joy, founder of mercy,
Who illumineth heaven and earth thereby,
Hear my clamorous complaint, though late it be,
Receive my prayers, unworthy in this heavy life!
Though I be a sinner most abominable, 595
Yet let my name be written in Moses' table.

O Mary, pray to the Maker of everything
To vouchsafe me help at my ending,
And save me from the power of my enemy,
For Death assaileth me strongly! — 600
And, Lady, that I may, by means of thy prayer,
In your Son's glory as partner share,
Through the mediation of his passion I it crave.
I beseech you, help my soul to save!

Knowledge, give me the scourge of penance; 605
My flesh therewith shall give acquittance.
I will now begin, if God give me grace.

Knowledge.

Everyman, God give you time and space!
Thus I bequeath you into the hands of our Saviour,
Now may you make your reckoning sure. 610

Everyman.

In the name of the Holy Trinity,
My body sorely punished shall be.
Take this, body, for the sin of the flesh.
As thou delightest to go gay and fresh,
And in the way of damnation thou didst me bring,   615
Therefore suffer now the strokes of punishing.
Now of penance to wade the water clear I desire,
To save me from purgatory, that sharp fire.

Good Deeds.

I thank God now I can walk and go,
And am delivered of my sickness and woe!   620
Therefore with Everyman I will go and not spare;
His good works I will help him to declare.

Knowledge.

Now, Everyman, be merry and glad,
Your Good Deeds cometh now, ye may not be sad.
Now is your Good Deeds whole and sound,   625
Going upright upon the ground.

     [*Good Deeds rises and walks to them.*

Everyman.

My heart is light and shall be evermore.
Now will I smite faster than I did before.

Good Deeds.

Everyman, pilgrim, my special friend,
Blessed be thou without end!   630
For thee is prepared the eternal glory.
Now thou hast made me whole and sound this tide,
In every hour I will by thee abide.

Everyman.

Welcome, my Good Deeds! Now I hear thy voice,
  I weep for sweetness of love.   635

Knowledge.

Be no more sad, but ever rejoice!
  God seeth thy manner of life on his throne above.
  Put on this garment to thy behoof,
Which wet with the tears of your weeping is,
Or else in God's presence you may it miss,   640
When ye to your journey's end come shall.

Everyman.

Gentle Knowledge, what do you it call?

Knowledge.

A garment of sorrow it is by name,
From pain it will you reclaim.
Contrition it is,   645
That getteth forgiveness,
Passing well it doth God please.

Good Deeds.

Everyman, will you wear it for your soul's ease?

[*Everyman puts on the robe of contrition.*

Everyman.

Now blessed be Jesu, Mary's son,
For now have I on true contrition!   650
And let us go now without tarrying.
Good Deeds, have we all clear our reckoning?

Good Deeds.

Yea, indeed, I have them here.

Everyman.

Then I trust we need not fear.
Now, friends, let us not part in twain!   655

Knowledge.

Nay, Everyman, that will we not, for certain.

Good Deeds.

Yet must thou lead with thee
  Three persons of great might.

Everyman.

Who should they be ?

Good Deeds.

Discretion and Strength they hight.   660
And thy Beauty may not abide behind.

Knowledge.

Also ye must call to mind
Your Five Wits as your counsellors beside.

Good Deeds.

You must have them ready at every tide.

Everyman.

How shall I get them hither ?   665

Knowledge.

You must call them all together,
And they will hear you immediately.

Everyman.

My friends, come hither and present be,
Discretion, Strength, my Five Wits, and Beauty.

[*They enter.*

Beauty.

Here at your will be we all ready.   670
What will ye that we should do ?

Good Deeds.

That ye should with Everyman go,
And help him in his pilgrimage.
Advise you — will you with him or not, on that voyage ?

Strength.

We will all bring him thither,   675
To help him and comfort, believe ye me !

Discretion.

So will we go with him all together.

Everyman.

Almighty God, beloved mayest thou be!
I give thee praise that I have hither brought
Strength, Discretion, Beauty, Five Wits — lack I
    nought —   680
And my Good Deeds, with Knowledge clear,
All be in my company at my will here.
I desire no more in this my anxiousness.

Strength.

And I, Strength, will stand by you in your distress,
Though thou wouldest in battle fight on the ground. 685

Five Wits.

And though it were through the world round,
We will not leave you for sweet or sour.

Beauty.

No more will I unto Death's hour,
Whatsoever thereof befall.

Discretion.

Everyman, advise you first of all.   690
Go with a good advisement and deliberation.
We all give you virtuous monition
That all shall be well.

Everyman.

My friends, hearken what I will tell.
I pray God reward you in his heavenly sphere.   695
Now hearken all that be here,
For I will make my testament
Here before you all present.
    In alms, half my goods will I give with my hands
        twain,
In the way of charity with good intent,   700
    And the other half still shall remain
In bequest to return where it ought to be.

This I do in despite of the fiend of hell,
Out of his peril to quit me well
For ever after and this day.   705

Knowledge.

Everyman, hearken what I say.
Go to Priesthood, I you advise,
And receive of him in any wise
The Holy Sacrament and Unction together,
Then see ye speedily turn again hither.   710
We will all await you here, verily.

Five Wits.

Yea, Everyman, haste thee that ye may ready be.
There is no emperor, king, duke, nor baron bold,
That from God such commission doth hold
As he doth to the least priest in this world consign, 715
For of the Blessed Sacraments, pure and benign,
He beareth the keys, and thereof hath the cure
For man's redemption, it is ever sure,
Which God as medicine for our souls' gain
Gave us out of his heart with great pain,   720
Here in this transitory life for thee and me.
Of the Blessed Sacraments seven there be,
Baptism, Confirmation, with Priesthood good,
And the Sacrament of God's precious Flesh and Blood,
Marriage, the Holy Extreme Unction, and Penance. 725
These seven are good to have in remembrance,
Gracious Sacraments of high divinity.

Everyman.

Fain would I receive that holy body.
And meekly to my spiritual father will I go.

Five Wits.

Everyman, that is best that ye can do.   730
God will you to salvation bring,

For Priesthood exceedeth every other thing.
To us Holy Scripture they do teach,
And convert men from sin, heaven to reach.
God hath to them more power given   735
Than to any angel that is in heaven.
With five words he may consecrate
God's body in flesh and blood to make,
And handleth his Maker between his hands.
The priest bindeth and unbindeth all bands   740
Both in earth and heaven. —
Thou dost administer all the Sacraments seven.
Though we should kiss thy feet, yet thereof thou worthy
    wert.
Thou art the surgeon that doth cure of mortal sin the
    hurt.
Remedy under God we find none   745
Except in Priesthood alone. —
Everyman, God gave priests that dignity,
And setteth them in his stead among us to be,
Thus be they above angels in degree.

Knowledge.

If priests be good, it is so surely;   750
But when Jesus hung on the cross with grievous smart,
There he gave out of his blessed heart
That same Sacrament in grievous torment. —
He sold them not to us, that Lord omnipotent.
Therefore Saint Peter the apostle doth say   755
That Jesus' curse have all they
Which God their Saviour do buy or sell,
Or if they for any money do " take or tell."
Sinful priests give sinners bad example in deed and
    word,
Their children sit by other men's fires, I have heard, 760

And some haunt of women the company,
With life unclean as through lustful acts of lechery —
These be with sin made blind.

Five Wits.

I trust to God no such may we find.
Therefore let us do Priesthood honor,　　　　　765
And follow their doctrines for our souls' succor.
We be their sheep, and they shepherds be,
By whom we all are kept in security.
Peace! for yonder I see Everyman come,
Who unto God hath made true satisfaction.　　　770

Good Deeds.

Methinketh it is he indeed.

Everyman.

Now may Jesus all of you comfort and speed!
I have received the Sacrament for my redemption,
And also mine extreme unction.
Blessed be all they that counselled me to take it! 775
And now, friends, let us go without longer respite.
I thank God ye would so long waiting stand.
Now set each of you on this rood your hand,
And shortly follow me.
I go before where I would be.　　　　　　　780
God be our guide!

Strength.

Everyman, we will not from you go,
　Till ye have gone this voyage long.

Discretion.

I, Discretion, will abide by you also.

Knowledge.

And though of this pilgrimage the hardships be
　never so strong,　　　　　　　　　785
No turning backward in me shall you know.

Everyman, I will be as sure by thee,
As ever I was by Judas Maccabee.

Everyman.

Alas! I am so faint I may not stand,
  My limbs under me do fold.   790
Friends, let us not turn again to this land,
  Not for all the world's gold,
For into this cave must I creep,
And turn to the earth, and there sleep.

Beauty.

What — into this grave! Alas! Woe is me!   795

Everyman.

Yea, there shall ye consume utterly.

Beauty.

And what, — must I smother here?

Everyman.

Yea, by my faith, and never more appear!
In this world we shall live no more at all,
But in heaven before the highest lord of all.   800

Beauty.

I cross out all this! Adieu, by Saint John!
I take " my tap in my lap " and am gone.

Everyman.

What, Beauty! — whither go ye?

Beauty.

Peace! I am deaf, I look not behind me,
Not if thou wouldest give me all the gold in thy
    chest.   805

    ⌈*Beauty goes, followed by the others, as they
      speak in turn.*

Everyman.

Alas! in whom may I trust!

Beauty fast away from me doth hie.
She promised with me to live and die.

Strength.

Everyman, I will thee also forsake and deny,
Thy game liketh me not at all!   810

Everyman.

Why, then ye will forsake me all!
Sweet Strength, tarry a little space.

Strength.

Nay, Sir, by the rood of grace,
I haste me fast my way from thee to take,
Though thou weep till thy heart do break.   815

Everyman.

Ye would ever abide by me, ye said.

Strength.

Yea, I have you far enough conveyed.
Ye be old enough, I understand,
Your pilgrimage to take in hand.
I repent me that I thither came.   820

Everyman.

Strength, for displeasing you I am to blame.
Will ye break " promise that is debt " ?

Strength.

In faith, I care not!
Thou art but a fool to complain,
You spend your speech and waste your brain.   825
Go, thrust thyself into the ground!

Everyman.

I had thought more sure I should you have found,
But I see well, who trusteth in his Strength,
She him deceiveth at length.
Both Strength and Beauty have forsaken me,   830
Yet they promised me fair and lovingly.

Discretion.

Everyman, I will after Strength be gone —
As for me, I will leave you alone.

Everyman.

Why, Discretion, will ye forsake me!

Discretion.

Yea, in faith, I will go from thee,   835
For when Strength goeth before
I follow after, evermore.

Everyman.

Yet, I pray thee, for love of the Trinity
Look in my grave once in pity of me.

Discretion.

Nay, so nigh will I not come, trust me well!   840
Now I bid you each farewell.

Everyman.

Oh, all things fail save God alone —
Beauty, Strength, and Discretion!
For when Death bloweth his blast,
They all run from me full fast.   845

Five Wits.

Everyman, my leave now of thee I take.
I will follow the others, for here I thee forsake.

Everyman.

Alas! then may I wail and weep,
   For I took you for my best friend.

Five Wits.

I will thee no longer keep.   850
   Now farewell, and here 's an end!

Everyman.

O Jesu, help! All have forsaken me.

Good Deeds.

Nay, Everyman, I will abide by thee,
  I will not forsake thee indeed!
  Thou wilt find me a good friend at need.   855

Everyman.

Gramercy, Good Deeds, now may I true friends see.
They have forsaken me everyone,
I loved them better than my Good Deeds alone.
Knowledge, will ye forsake me also?

Knowledge.

Yea, Everyman, when ye to death shall go,   860
But not yet, for no manner of danger.

Everyman.

Gramercy, Knowledge, with all my heart!

Knowledge.

Nay, yet will I not from hence depart,
Till whereunto ye shall come, I shall see and know.

Everyman.

Methinketh, alas! that I must now go   865
To make my reckoning, and my debts pay,
For I see my time is nigh spent away.
Take example, all ye that this do hear or see,
How they that I love best do forsake me,
Except my Good Deeds that abideth faithfully.   870

Good Deeds.

All earthly things are but vanity.
Beauty, Strength and Discretion do man forsake,
Foolish friends and kinsmen that fair spake,
All flee away save Good Deeds, and that am I!

Everyman.

Have mercy on me, God most mighty,   875
And stand by me, thou Mother and Maid, holy Mary!

Good Deeds.

Fear not, I will speak for thee.

Everyman.

Here I cry God mercy!

Good Deeds.

Shorten our end and minish our pain,
Let us go and never come again. 880

Everyman.

Into thy hands, Lord, my soul I commend —
   Receive it, Lord, that it be not lost!
As thou didst me buy, so do thou me defend,
   And save me from the fiend's boast
That I may appear with that blessed host 885
That shall be saved at the day of doom.
   In manus tuas, of mights the most,
Forever *commendo spiritum meum.*

           [*Everyman goes into the grave.*

Knowledge.

Now that he hath suffered that we all shall endure,
The Good Deeds shall make all sure; 890
Now that he hath made ending,
Methinketh that I hear angels sing,
And make great joy and melody,
Where Everyman's soul shall received be!

           [*The Angel appears.*

The Angel.

Come, excellent elect spouse to Jesu! 895
   Here above shalt thou go,
Because of thy singular virtue.
   Now thy soul from thy body is taken, lo!
Thy reckoning is crystal clear.
Now shalt thou into the heavenly sphere, 900

Unto which ye all shall come
That live well before the day of doom.

[The Angel goes and the Doctor enters.
Doctor.

Doctor.

This moral men may have in mind, —
　Ye hearers, take it as of worth, both young and old,
And forsake Pride, for he deceiveth you in the end,
　　　as ye will find,   905
　　And remember Beauty, Five Wits, Strength, and
　　　Discretion, all told,
They all at the last do Everyman forsake
Save that his Good Deeds there doth he take.
But beware, if they be small,
Before God he hath no help at all,   910
None excuse for Everyman may there then be there.
Alas, how shall he then do and fare !
For after death amends may no man make,
For then Mercy and Pity do him forsake.
If his reckoning be not clear when he doth come,   915
God will say, *Ite, maledicti, in ignem æternum.*
And he that hath his account whole and sound,
High in heaven he shall be crowned,
Unto which place God bring us all thither
That we may live, body and soul, together !   920
Thereto their aid vouchsafe the Trinity —
Amen, say ye, for holy Charity !

FINIS.

Thus endeth this moral play of Everyman.

THE ROBIN HOOD PLAYS

[THE following plays may be found in Child's *English and Scottish Popular Ballads*, vol. iii, 90, 114, 127, and in Manly's *Specimens of the Pre-Shaksperean Drama*, vol. i, 279, 281, 285. The first is from a fragment, consisting of a loose half-leaf evidently torn from a folio MS., in the possession of Dr. W. Aldis Wright. Certain memoranda upon the back of this leaf indicate the play to be earlier than 1475. The two others were originally printed as a single play by Copeland about 1550 and by White in 1634. They were reprinted by Ritson in his *Robin Hood*, 1795. Child gave variant readings from White, and Manly includes with these Ritson's readings, and Copeland's readings as given by Ritson. See Child and Manly, *ut supra*.]

I

ROBIN HOOD AND THE KNIGHT

[*Knight.*]
Sir Sheriff, for thy sake,
Robin Hood will I take.

[*Sheriff.*]
I will give thee gold and fee,
This promise if thou keep to me.

[*The Knight meets Robin and challenges him to shoot.*

[*Knight.*]

Robin Hood, fair and free,   **5**
Under this linden shoot we.

[*Robin.*]

With thee shoot I will,
All thy pleasures to fulfill.

[*Knight.*]

Have at the prick!

[*Robin.*]

And I cleave the stick!   **10**

[*Knight.*]

Let us cast the stone.

[*Robin.*]

I assent gladly, by Saint John.

[*They cast the stone, Robin is victorious, and is
again challenged.*]

[*Knight.*]

Let us cast the axle-tree.

[*Robin.*]

Have a foot before thee!

[*They wrestle, and the Knight is thrown.*]

[*Robin.*]

Sir Knight, ye have a fall!   **15**

[*Knight.*]

And I shall requite thee, Robin, for all!
Out upon thee! I blow my horn —

[*Robin.*]

It were better to be unborn!
Let us fight at outrance.[1]

---

[1] *At outrance:* to the extremity, to the death.

[*Knight.*]

He that fleeth, God give him mischance.   20
    [*Robin slays him, and puts on his clothes.*

[*Robin.*]

Now *I* have the mastery here,
This sorry neck I smite off sheer.
This knight's clothes will I wear,
And in my hood his head will bear.

    [*Robin meets a man who tells him his men are
    being worsted by the Sheriff.*

[*Robin.*]

Well met, my fellow, well met now!   25
Of good Robin what hearest thou?

[*Man.*]

Robin Hood and his company
By the Sheriff taken be.

[*Robin.*]

Haste we then, with good will,
And the Sheriff will we kill.   30
    [*They view the fight apart.*

Just look ye now on Friar Tuck,
How he doth his bow pluck!

[*Sheriff.*]

Sirs, to the Sheriff now yield ye,
Or else your bows shall broken be!

[*An Outlaw.*]

Now be we all bound in sorry sort.   35
Friar Tuck, this is no sport!
    [*The Sheriff calls upon Robin's men to surrender.*

[*Sheriff.*]

Come thou forth, thou false outlaw,
We shall thee hang and draw!

[*Friar Tuck.*]

Now, alas, what shall we do!
We must to the prison go.

    [*Robin's men are taken to the prison.*
     [*Sheriff.*]

Open the gates without delay,
And see that these thieves go in straightway! . . .

II

ROBIN HOOD AND THE POTTER

Robin Hood.

Listen to me, my merry men all,   [121]
  And hark what I shall say —
Of an adventure I shall you tell
  That befell this other day.
With a proud potter I met,   5
And a rose-garland on his head ; —
The flowers of it shone marvellous fresh.
  This seven year and more he hath used this way,
Yet was he never so courteous a potter
  As one penny passage to pay.   10 [130]
Is there any of my merry men all
  That dare be so bold
To make the potter pay passage
  Either silver or gold?

Little John.

Not I, master, for twenty pound ready told, 15 [135]
  For there is not, among us all, one
That dare fight with that potter, man for man.
  I felt his hands not long agone,

But I had liefer been here by thee,
Therefore I know what he is. 20 [140]
Meet him when ye will, or meet him when ye shall,
He is as proper a man as ever you fought with, withal.

Robin Hood.

I will lay with thee, Little John, twenty pound so red
If I with that potter meet,
I will make him pay passage, maugre his head.[1] 25 [145]

Little John.

I consent thereto, so eat I bread!
If he pay passage, maugre his head,
Twenty pound will I give you for meed,[2] well sped.

[*They go, leaving Robin. Jack, the Potter's boy,*
enters.

The Potter's Boy Jack.

Out upon it that ever I saw this day!
For I am clean out of my way 30 [150]
From Nottingham town.
If I hie me not the faster,
Ere I come there, the market will be done.

Robin Hood.

Let me see, are the pots whole and sound?

Jack.

Yea, master, but they will not break the ground. 35 [155]

Robin Hood.

I will them break, for the cuckold, thy master's sake,
And if they will break the ground,
Thou shalt have threepence for a pound.

[*He dashes the pots to the ground.*

---

[1] *Maugre his head* (so also *face, eyes, teeth,* etc.): in spite of all he
can do.
[2] Reward.

Jack.

Out upon it, alas, what have ye done !

If my master comes, he will break your crown.   40 [160]

[*The Potter enters.*
The Potter.

Why, thou whoreson, art thou here yet ?

Thou shouldest have been at market.

Jack.

I met with Robin Hood, a good yeoman.

He hath broken my pots,

And called you cuckold by your name.   45 [16o]

The Potter.

Thou mayest be a gentleman, so God me save,

But thou seemest a naughty knave.

Thou callest me cuckold by my name,

And I swear by God and Saint John,

Wife had I never none —   50 [170]

This cannot I deny.

But if thou be a good fellow,

I will sell my horse, my harness, pots and panniers too,

Thou shalt have the one half, and I will have the other.

If thou be not so content,   55 [175]

Thou shalt have stripes, though thou wert my brother.

Robin Hood.

Hark, potter, what I shall say.

This seven year and more thou hast used this way,

Yet wert thou never so courteous to me

As one penny passage to pay.   60 [180]

The Potter.

Why should I pay passage to thee ?

Robin Hood.

For I am Robin Hood, chief governor

Under the greenwood tree.

The Potter.

This seven year have I used this way up and down,
Yet paid I passage to no man, 65 [18▪
Not now I will not begin; though thou do the worst
  thou can.

Robin Hood.

Passage shalt thou pay here under the greenwood tree,
Or else thou shalt leave a pledge with me.

The Potter.

If thou be a good fellow, as men do thee call,
Lay away thy bow, 70 [190]
And take thy sword and buckler in thy hand,
And see what shall befall.

Robin Hood.

Little John, where art thou?

Little [*John.*]

Here, master, I make to God my vow,
I told you, master, so God me save, 75 [194]
That you should find the potter a knave.
Hold your buckler fast in your hand,
And I will stiffly by you stand,
Ready for to fight.
Be the knave never so stout, 80 [200]
I shall rap him on the snout,
And put him to flight. . . .
  [*The rest of the play is wanting.*]

III

ROBIN HOOD AND THE FRIAR

Robin Hood.

Now stand ye forth, my merry men all,
 And hark what I shall say —,

Of an adventure I shall you tell,
    The which befell this other day.
    As I went by the high-way,   5
With a stout friar I met,
    And a quarter-staff in his hand,
Lightly to me he lept,
    And still he bade me stand.
There were strokes two or three,   10
    But I cannot tell who had the worse,
But well I wot the whoreson came in upon me,
    And from me he took my purse.
Is there any of my merry men all
    That to that friar will go,   15
And bring him to me forthwithal,[1]
    Whether he will or no ?

Little John.

Yea, master, I make to God my vow,
    To that friar will I go,
And bring him to you now,   20
    Whether he will or no.

[*They go. Friar Tuck enters with three dogs.*

Friar Tuck.

Deus hic ! Deus hic ! God be here !
Is not this a holy word for a frere ?[2]
God save all this company !
    But am not I a jolly friar?   25
For I can shoot both far and near,
And handle the sword and buckler,
And this quarter-staff also.
If I meet with a gentleman or yeoman,
I am not afraid to look him upon,   30

[1] Forthwith.   [2] Friar.

Nor boldly with him to carp;[1]
If he speak any words to me,
He shall have stripes two or three
   That shall make his body smart.
But, masters, to show you the matter   35
Wherefore and why.I am come hither,
In faith I will not spare.
I am come to seek a good yeoman,
In Bernisdale men say is his habitation,
His name is Robin Hood.   40
And if that he be better man than I,
His servant will I be and serve him truly,
But if that I be better man than he,
By my truth, my knave shall he be,
And lead these dogs all three.   45

       [*Robin enters and takes him by the throat.*

       Robin Hood.
Yield thee, friar, in thy long coat!
       Friar Tuck.
I beshrew [2] thy heart, knave — thou hurtest my throat !
       Robin Hood.
I trow, friar, thou beginnest to dote!
Who made thee so malapert and so bold
To come into this forest here   50
Among my fallow-deer?
       Friar.
Go louse [3] thee, ragged knave !
   If thou make many words, I will give it thee on the
       ear,

---

[1] Speak.   [2] Curse.
[3] Louse, to clear (one's self or another) of lice. The practice was one
of frequent necessity apparently until a comparatively modern period ;
the remark, however, is none the less insulting.

Though I be but a poor friar, —
　To seek Robin Hood I come here,　　　　　　　55
And to him my heart to unfold.
Robin Hood.
Thou lousy friar, what wouldest thou with him?
He never loved friar, nor none of friar's kin.
Friar Tuck.
Avaunt, ye ragged knave,
Or ye shall get it on the skin!　　　　　　　60
Robin Hood.
Of all the men on a morning thou art the worst!
To meet with thee I have no lust.[1]
For he that meeteth a friar or a fox in the morning,
To speed ill that day he standeth in jeopardy.
Therefore I had liefer meet with the devil of hell — 65
　Friar, I tell thee as I think! —
Than meet with a friar or a fox
　In a morning ere I drink.
Friar Tuck.
Avaunt, thou ragged knave! this is but a mock.
If thou make many words, thou shalt have a knock. 70
Robin Hood.
Hark, friar, what I say here.
Over this water thou shalt me bear,
The bridge is borne away.
Friar Tuck.
To say nay I will not ;
To prevent thee from thine oath were great pity and
　　sin,　　　　　　　　　　　　　　　75
So up upon a friar's back, and have straightway in !
Robin Hood.
Nay, have over!
　　　　　　[*He gets upon the Friar's back.*
　　　[1] Desire.

Friar.

Now am I, friar, within, and thou, Robin, without,
To lay thee here I have no great doubt.

        [The Friar throws him into the stream.

Now am I, friar, without, and thou, Robin, within. 8C
Lie there, knave! Choose whether thou wilt sink or
    swim!

Robin Hood.

Why, thou lousy friar, what hast thou done!

Friar.

Marry, set a knave above his shoon! [1]

Robin Hood.

And for that thou shalt suffer!

        [He makes towards the Friar.

Friar.

Why, wilt thou fight a pluck? [2]   85

Robin Hood.

And God send me good luck!

Friar.

Then have a stroke for Friar Tuck!

        [They fight.

Robin Hood.

Hold thy hand, friar, and hear me speak!

Friar.

Say on, ragged knave,
  Me seemeth ye begin to sweat.   9C

Robin Hood.

In this forest I have a hound,
I will not give him for a hundred pound.
Give me leave my horn to blow,
That my hound may know.

---

[1] Shoes.   [2] Bout, set-to.

Friar.

Blow on, ragged knave, without any doubt,   95
Until both thine eyes start out.

> [*Robin blows, and his men enter.*

Here be a sort of ragged knaves come in,
Clothed all in Kendal green,
And to thee they take their way now.

Robin Hood.

Peradventure they do so.   100

Friar.

I gave thee leave to blow at thy will,
Now give me leave to whistle my fill.

Robin Hood.

Whistle, friar, evil may thou fare,
Until both thine eyes stare.

> [*The Friar whistles and his men enter.*

Friar.

Now, Cut and Bause,   105
Bring forth the clubs and staves,
And down with those ragged knaves!

> [*They fight, until Robin gestures for a pause.*

Robin Hood.

How sayest thou, friar, wilt thou be my man,
To do me the best service thou can?
Thou shalt have both gold and fee,   110
And also here is a lady free,
I will give her unto thee,
And her chaplain I thee make
To serve her for my sake.

[*In the seven lines, best omitted, which conclude
the fragments, the Friar accepts, bidding his men go
home " and lay crabs in the fire," and expressing
his delight in Robin's proposal.*]

THE OXFORDSHIRE SAINT GEORGE
PLAY

[The following mummers' play was printed first in
Notes and Queries, 5th series, vol. ii, 503 ff. (Dec. 26,
1874), by the Rev. Dr. Frederick George Lee, under
the title "Oxfordshire Christmas Miracle Play." It
is also printed by Manly in his *Specimens of the Pre-
Shaksperean Drama*, vol. i, 289. Dr. Lee wrote of it
as follows: "The text of the play was taken down by
myself from the lips of one of the performers in 1853.
I first saw it acted in the Hall of the old Vicarage
House at Thame, in the year 1839, by those whose
custom it had been, from time immemorial, to perform
it at the houses of the gentle-folk of that neighbour-
hood at Christmas, between St. Thomas's Day and
Old Christmas Eve, January 5. These performers
(now long scattered, and all dead but one, as I am
informed) claimed to be the 'true and legitimate
successors' of the mummers who, in previous centuries, constantly performed at the 'Whitsun' and
'Christmas Church Ales,' records of which are
found on almost every page of the 'Stewards' and
Churchwardens' Books of the Prebendal Church of
our Blessed Lady of Thame.' In Mr. Lupton's *History of Thame,* some account of these performances is
given ; while, in the 'Address' prefixed to his pri-
vately-printed and curious tract, *Extracts from the
Accounts of the Proctors and Stewards,* &c., of that
town, he refers to the exceeding popularity of the

mumming for many years. In Lord Wenham's time,
i. e. 1790, the performances were annually given at
Thame Park; and at the Baronial Hall of Brill,
Bucks, about 1808-14, the entertainment was attended
by the nobility and gentry for miles round, and is
reported to have been produced on a scale of consider-
able magnificence. The man from whom I took down
the following in my notebook had performed at Brill,
in the year 1807, and his father had done the same
at Thame Park in the previous century. I do not pro-
fess to be able to explain the text of the play, nor
can I quite admire all its points. Its coarseness, too,
is not to my taste. Least of all can I comprehend its
purport. Its anachronisms will be patent to all. But
at least its action is vigorous, and, when I was a boy, I
confess that I thought the performance most delightful
and impressive. As the late Mr. Lupton (a local anti-
quarian and a gentleman of excellent taste. and high
character) informed me of so much that is here set
forth, I may add that he, at the same time, expressed
his conviction that my version of the play is most
probably the only one that had ever been committed
to paper; for the dialogue was purely traditional, and
handed down from father to son. Nothing whatsoever
has been altered or added by myself. I have only
ventured to put the directions in Italics in a little
more concise and intelligible language than that in
which they were dictated to me."

Mr. Chambers in his *Medieval Stage* devotes a
chapter to the Saint George Play (vol. i, 205 ff.), listing
twenty-seven printed versions on which his account is
based. The play is distinctively a play, with characters playing individual parts, as distinguished from the

various sword and other dances which sometimes include dramatic features, but with few and indefinite
characters, a connecting feature being that in some
cases in the dances a doctor appears as in the Saint
George Play. This play seems far to have surpassed
other forms of mummers' play in popularity. For the
general subject of folk-plays, see the volume announced
by the Folk-Lore Society under the editorship of
T. F. Ordish, who has already treated it in *Folk-Lore*,
vol. ii, 326, vol. iv, 162.

The play consists characteristically of three parts, the
"presentation," in which the persons, as they are successively announced, come forward or "enter" from the
half circle in which they stand; the "drama" proper;
and the "quete," or passing round a suitable receptacle
for gifts of money, which terminates the performance.
The serious presentation of the story of Saint George,
forming the kernel of the play, has, as will be seen,
long since merged in rustic burlesque and foolery,
for which Dr. Lee felt it necessary to offer his quaint
apology. That the story should have been turned into
extravaganza was inevitable, if it was to be perpetuated
at all, after its original inspiration had disappeared with
the conditions of life and belief which originated and
fostered it. Degenerate and intrinsically trivial as the
modern versions of these plays are, they are, however,
of real interest and value in illustrating the persistence
of tradition, and above all as attesting the natural
tendency of popular drama to turn to national tradition
and history for themes for dramatic presentation.

The many versions vary widely in minor details,
though alike in outline. There is great variety as regards the names of the characters, even Saint George,

who in some versions would be quite unrecognizable
were it not for the parallel afforded by other versions.
The version here printed seems rather more full and
interesting than others. Manly prints another modern
version (the " Lutterworth "), and another from Corn-
wall may be found in " *Everyman* " *with other Interludes* in " Everyman's Library," Appendix A.

The text here given reproduces Dr. Lee's text in
Notes and Queries, following it in arrangement of
lines, explanation of words, and other details.

DRAMATIS PERSONÆ

KING ALFRED	OLD FATHER CHRISTMAS
KING ALFRED's QUEEN	ST. GEORGE OF ENGLAND
KING WILLIAM	THE OLD DRAGON
OLD KING COLE (WITH A WOODEN LEG)	THE MERRY ANDREW
GIANT BLUNDERBORE	OLD DOCTOR BALL
LITTLE JACK	MORRES-MEN

*All the mummers come in singing, and walk round the
place in a circle, and then stand on one side.*

Enter King Alfred and his Queen arm-in-arm.
I am King Alfred, and this here is my Bride.
I 've a crown on my pate and a sword by my side.
[*Stands apart.*

Enter King Cole.
I am King Cole, and I carry my stump.
Hurrah for King Charles! down with old Noll's Rump!
[*Stands apart.*

Enter King William.
I am King William of blessed me-mo-ry,
Who came and pulled down the high gallows-tree,
And brought us all peace and pros-pe-ri-ty.
[*Stands apart.*

Enter Giant Blunderbore.

I am Giant Blunderbore, fee, fi, fum,
Ready to fight ye all — so I says, " Come ! "

> *[Enter Little Jack.*

And this here is my little man Jack,
A thump on his rump and a whack on his back !

> *[Strikes him twice.*

I 'll fight King Alfred, I 'll fight King Cole,
I 'm ready to fight any mortal soul ;
So here I, Blunderbore, takes my stand,
With this little devil, Jack, at my right hand,
Ready to fight for mortal life. Fee, fi, fum.

> *[The Giant and Little Jack stand apart.*

Enter St. George.

I am St. George of Merry Eng-land,
Bring in the morres-men, bring in our band.

> *[Morres-men come forward and dance to a tune
> from fife and drum. The dance being ended,
> St. George continues :*

These are our tricks. Ho ! men, ho !
These are our sticks, — whack men so !

> *[Strikes the Dragon, who roars, and comes for-
> ward.*

The Dragon speaks.

Stand on head, stand on feet !
Meat, meat, meat for to eat !

> *[Tries to bite King Alfred.*

I am the dragon, here are my jaws,
I am the dragon, here are my claws.
Meat, meat, meat for to eat !
Stand on my head, stand on my feet !

> *[Turns a summersault and stands aside.*

All sing, several times repeated.

Ho! ho! ho!

Whack men so!

[*The drum and fife sound. They all fight, and after general disorder, fall down.*

Old Dr. Ball comes forward.

I am the Doctor and I cure all ills,

Only gullup my portions [*qy.* potions] and swallow my pills;

I can cure the itch, the stitch, the pox, the palsy and the gout,

All pains within and all pains without.

Up from the floor, Giant Blunderbore!

[*Gives him a pill, and he rises at once.*

Get up, King; get up, Bride;

Get up, Fool, and stand aside.

[*Gives them each a pill, and they rise.*

Get up, King Cole, and tell the gentlefolks all

There never was a doctor like Mr. Doctor Ball.

Get up, St. George, old England's knight,

[*Gives him a pill.*

You have wounded the Dragon and finished the fight.

[*All stand aside but the Dragon, who lies in convulsions on the floor.*

Now kill the old Dragon and poison old Nick.

At Yule-tyde, both o' ye, cut your stick!

[*The doctor forces a large pill down the Dragon's throat, who thereupon roars, and dies in convulsions.*

Then enter Father Christmas.

Father Christmas.

I am Father Christmas! hold, men, hold!

Be there loaf in your locker, and sheep in your fold,

A fire on the hearth, and good luck for your lot,
Money in your pocket, and a pudding in the pot !

He sings.
　Hold, men, hold !
　Put up your sticks,
　End all your tricks ;
　Hold, men, hold !

[*Chorus (all sing while one goes round with a
　hat for gifts).*
　　Hold, men, hold !
　　We are very cold,
　　Inside and outside,
　　We are very cold.
　　If you don't give us silver,
　　Then give us gold
From the money in your pockets —
　[*Some of the performers show signs of fighting
　again.*
　　Hold, men, hold !

Song and chorus.
God A'mighty bless your hearth and fold,
Shut out the wolf and keep out the cold ;
You gev' [have given] us silver, keep you the gold,
For 't is money in your pocket. — Hold, men, hold !

Repeat in chorus.
God A'mighty bless, &c.

　　　　　　　[*Exeunt omnes.*

NOTES

THE ENGLISH *QUEM QUÆRITIS*

1. **Parasceve day.** Good Friday, a specific use of *Parasceve* (Late Latin *parasceve*, from Greek παρασκευή, preparation, in Jewish use, day of preparation), the day of preparation for the Jewish sabbath, the eve of the sabbath, namely Friday. See the *Oxford Dictionary*.

2. **Tenebræ.** Matins and Lauds of the following day sung at this season during the afternoon of the day previous.

3. **Prime.** One of the " canonical hours " for daily service, the use of which, since the Reformation, is limited practically to the Roman Communion. The hours have varied at various times, one or more of the services being performed together. The more important hours, as observed with some strictness, are Matins with Lauds, after midnight ; Prime, Tierce, Sext, and Nones, at the first, third, sixth, and ninth hour, beginning with six in the morning ; Vespers at about four ; Complin at some time after Vespers.

4. Here the ritual for the Adoration of the Cross begins.

5. Note the dramatic intention in this action.

6. Here the Deposition begins.

7. So called as celebrated with a Host consecrated at a previous service and reserved.

8. **thuribles.** Vessels for incense.

9. " Whom seek ye in the tomb, O lovers of Christ ? "

" Jesus of Nazareth, him that was crucified, O heavenly being."

" He is not here. He is risen, as he hath prophesied. Go, announce, that he hath risen from the dead."

" Alleluia, the Lord hath risen ! "

" Come and see the place where the Lord was placed. Alleluia, Alleluia !

" The Lord hath risen from the dead who hung for us upon the tree [wood]."

ABRAHAM AND ISAAC

16. I know *added.*
29. readiest: full ready.
30. Both early and late.
40. would . . . know: fell.
50. amain: certain.
54. might and main: all my main (might).
55. Full soon anon [Holthausen's emendation].
68. command: message.
72, 73. I had liefer, if God had been pleased, to have gone without all the good that I have.
79. the more: sore.
82. thereto *added.*
85. But do after my Lord's teaching.
86. great a deal: well.
92. look thou obey [Manly's emendation]: look that thou keep.
94. well paid [translating for rime *apayd,* "satisfied; pleased," Manly's emendation]: well pleased.
95. the best I may: to the best I have.
98. withhold my debt: let [i. e. "make opposition, resist, refuse"].
100. may be: we can.
123. might and main: all our might.
129. there: down.
132. was told: should.
139. by *added.*
146. Through his sweet sending.
154. thus *added.*
166. your son *added.*
169. God wot *added.*
174. it . . . please: I may not choose.
184. here *added.*
190. decree: will.
193. will [Manly's emendation]: pleasure.

200. no . . . renew : make you no grief.

208. My heart beginneth strongly to rise.

217. rise . . . stand : do thou up stand.

220. as may accord : on earth.

235. that I do *added.*

270. none : never once.

271. bone : bones.

274, 275. [The usual numbering is kept, though l. 274 is divided, as *morne* seems intended as rime for *born.*]

278. proceed : address myself.

279. In truth I had as lief myself slay.

283. as *added.*

286. so broad *added.*

299. Ah, Lord, my heart riseth thee against.

301. My heart will not now thereto.

308. no . . . know : done.

322. And some of thy heaviness to remove.

326. here . . . side : that here is.

350. [Use has been made here of Manly's emendation of the line division in the original which runs : No . . . son | For . . . sent | Hither . . . us | . The old numbering is retained, however, below (see l. 355) to preserve uniformity.]

368. [This line is divided into two lines at *sheep* in both of Miss Smith's editions. Hence, from here on, as in Manly's text, where the line division is corrected, the numbering of the lines is one behind Miss Smith's.]

379. No, surely, sweet son, have no dread.

381. indeed *added.*

411. so *added.*

419. Yea, come on with me, my own sweet son.

434. [It is the office of the "Doctor" in a miracle or morality to explain in prologue or epilogue the purpose or moral of the play.]

435. now, for example *added.*

439. God wot *added.*

440. clear : here.

441, 442. How we should keep to our power God's commandments without murmuring.

447. sirs . . . be; sirs, thereby.

451. As is nature and kind [i. e. natural law].

452. ye . . . trow: I may well avow.

458. Though ye be never so hard bestead.

460, 461. His commandments truly if ye keep with good heart. As this story hath now showed you before.

SECOND SHEPHERDS' PLAY

2. were the truth told *added*.

4. It is not as I would for I am all lapt.

10. shepherds. [So in original. Manly suggests *husbandys*, "husbandmen" (cf. l. 22), which would preserve the rime.]

15, 16. We are so "hamyd," over-taxed, and "ramyd." [The words *hamyd* (*hemmed* altered for the rime) and *ramyd* (presumably "rammed") are used indefinitely to suggest violence of action. The passage may therefore be loosely translated for the sake of the rime without injury to the author's intention.]

20. These men that are "lord-fest" [i. e. bound to a lord, referring, as the context seems to show, not to persons in a servile condition, but to the lord's agents employed to enforce his claims upon his tenants].

22. husbandmen. [The term *husbandys*, "husbandmen," is here probably used in the specialized Northern sense of "tenants."]

28. a man: he [used, as personal pronouns sometimes are in Middle English, as an indefinite pronoun. It was possibly the wish to find an antecedent for *he* which led Kölbing, without good reason, to suggest interchanging this stanza and the next].

47. and . . . moan: in manner of moan.

57. Lord, this weather [literally, "these weathers"] is

spiteful and the weather so keen [Manly suggests *winters* for the first *weders*, or *winds* for the second, citing l. 128].

67. Capel. [A humorous name for a hen.]

75. God knows they are led, *etc.*

79. All round *added.*

88. But so far as I know.

91. as to wooing: of wooing. [Kittredge suggests that *of wooing* is equivalent to "a-wooing." *Of*, however, may be regarded here as having its frequent sense "in respect to, as to".]

100. by my fire: for my mate. [The exigency of the rime must stand as excuse for this paraphrase.]

103. clearer and higher: full clear. [The phrase, ll. 103, 104, is probably proverbial, used in ironical reference to a hoarse, rough voice; cf. l. 416.]

109. "God look over the row!" [No satisfactory explanation has been offered for this phrase, obviously a proverbial exclamation.]

110. Yea, the devil be in thy maw, thus tarrying.

112. just before *added.*

113. Not far.

121. It is ever in doubt and brittle as glass.

132. These floods so they drown.

138. Yet . . . heart: Yet methinks my heart.

139. Ye . . . wights: Ye are two all wights. [One would like to regard *two all* as an idiomatic phrase, meaning "two such both" (i. e. shrews), akin to various Middle English phrases having the sense of "each and every one" (one and all, each and all, all and each, all and sundry, all and some, all both), but no direct support can be found for this conjecture. Failing this, Kittredge's emendation of *all* to *tall* (as used in ballads, etc., "a tall man of his hands") is a felicitous suggestion, and probably restores the original reading.]

140. below *added* [see l. 179].

141. But in full bad humor have I been. [The paraphrase is forced by the rime.]

147. cheat: hind [laborer, servant].

148. for meat *added*.

149. We have made it [i. e. our meal].

153. To eat if we had it.

156. We are oft wet and weary when master-men [i. e. our masters] sleep.

162. And pay us full late.

163. since . . . way: for the fare [fuss] that ye make.

172. for work *added*.

177. Left lorn : We ask.

186. Let me sing the tenor.

190. Now, Lord, for thy seven names, that made both moon and stars. [There are seven names in Rabbinical literature, El, Elohim, Adonai, YHWH (Jahveh), Ehyer-Asher-Ehyeh, Shaddai, Lebaot: see Hemingway, *Yale Studies*, 38. Hemingway did not find mention of seven names elsewhere in Christian literature. Jerome gives ten in one place, and Junilius eight.]

191. Well more than I can name, thy will, Lorde, of [in respect to, for] me lacks. [In the original, " Well mo then I can neven, / thi will, Lorde, of me tharnys." The line is difficult. Obviously it would seem as if " Well more than I can name " should be construed with " stars " of the previous line. In that case, it is hard to find a satisfactory meaning, or an acceptable emendation, for *tharnys*. The best solution seems to be to take *tharnys* in its simple sense with " Well mo," etc., as its object, though it is by no means impossible that it is used absolutely and pregnantly for "lacks grievously what I would wish," and the phrase " Well mo," etc., belongs to " starnes." For the use of *of*, compare the *Oxford Dictionary*. s. v. *of*, iv, 14.

192. I am all at odds: that disturbs often my brain.

193. might . . . dwell: were in heaven.

197, 198. [This speech probably belongs to Primus Pastor. Three times the shepherds in turn gird at Mak, except that Primus Pastor has no speech in the first round, unless the question in l. 195 be so considered. Moreover, its point is greatly improved if uttered by one of the shepherds.

The shepherds' speeches are wrongly attributed in various places.]

201. What! I am a yeoman, I tell you, of the King.

202. indeed *added*.

202. messenger: "sonde" [i. e. "message" used for "messenger"; see similar uses cited by Skeat, *Piers the Plowman*, note on l. 2, one of which is *message* for *messenger* in the MSS. of Chaucer's *Man of Law's Tale* (*hunte* for *hunter* is erroneously cited)].

207. Why, who be I?

208. Why make ye it so quaint? Mak, ye do wrong!

210. by . . . kill: Would the devil might him hang!

211. you'll . . . fill: make you all to suffer.

212. from me *added*.

215. southern tooth. [Implying deceit in Mak's mouth like that of South of England folk — the play being Northern, and deceit being proverbially attributed to the South by the North.]

216. flea. [A euphemism for the word actually used in the original.]

218. beat: hurt.

219. I greet you *added*.

220. Oh . . . you! can you now remember.

221. Shrew, joke away!

222. Thus late as thou goest.

224. God knows *added*.

226. and say *added*.

227. verily and night and day *added*.

228. My belly fares not well, it is out of state.

235. ask I *added*.

236. close *added*.

240. as may be: as she can.

241. And each year that comes to man.

244. But were I not more amiable and richer by far. [*Not* amended to *now*, as the sense seems plainly to demand.]

245. I were eaten out of house and of lodging.

246. by God's curse *added*.

247. There is none that trows or knows a worse.

248. Than I know.

251, 252. [I. e. "If I could but pay for her burial mass."]

253. I wot so tired to death is, *etc.*

254. I would sleep though I took less for my hire.

255. and forlorn *added.*

256. I am weary, clean spent with racing and running in the mire.

263, 264. Then might I prevent you, anon, of talking over what ye would, no doubt. [Two lines missing in this stanza.]

269. Now 't were time for a man that lacks what he would.

274. their **wrath** to tell: for to rail. [I. e. "Now 't were time for the shepherds, if they knew what I was up to, to rail."]

278 ff. [Mak's charm (which might readily be supposed to be a mere piece of foolery, or at most a rustic spell) has been explained as possibly due to his being adapted from a "favorite comic character, the conjuror and buffoon Mangis of the romance of the *Four Sons of Aymon*"; so Pollard, note on this line wrongly numbered 289.]

281. soon *added.*

282. Of **might**: aloud. [*Aloud* is a mere tag, used for convenience as the "bob" of the stanza.]

288. Was I never a shepherd, but now will I learn.

289. a heap *added.*

301. One that has been [busied as a] house-wife.

305. Good wife, open the "hek" [i. e. "door," properly the half of a divided door.]

306. I may let thee draw the latch.

307. Yea, then needest not reck of my long standing.

308. still *added.*

315. some day *added.*

336–340. Thou counsellest [well]! And I shall say thou wast lightened of a boy child this night. Now lucky for me was that bright day that ever I was born.

352. and . . . sand: and I "water fasting" [i. e. having nothing else to drink].

353. [This "talking across the footlights" was no doubt relished as keenly by a mediæval audience as similar asides to-day.]

361. so . . . aching: so my brows grow pale.

374. It is but a phantom, by the Rood.

375. Now God turn all to good.

378. for aye *added*.

381. perdie *added*.

382. Many thanks! [Either ironical to express his gratitude for his supposed wry neck, or possibly in return for an attempt on the part of one of the shepherds to straighten it out for him.]

383. Stephen: "Strevyn."

385. " My hart out of-sloghe." [The meaning of *of-sloghe* is obscure. The rendering used must not be regarded as a translation, but merely a paraphrase giving the general sense.]

389. "tow on my rock more than ever I had " [i. e. more tow on my distaff to spin than ever before — more to look out for.]

391. banes: "tharnes" [i. e. *thernes*, servant-maids, literally, but also, as here, employed as an indefinite term of reproach, like *varlet*, *wench*, in later use.]

393. Wo is him has many children.

396. sleeve. [The full long sleeve was used as a pocket.]

402. Daw *added*.

403. thorn. [See note on l. 455.]

405. "walk in the wenyand." [Literally, " walk in the waning [moon]," i. e. "go where bad luck may attend you "; see Skeat, *Etymological Dictionary ;* a variant of the phrase is " with a wanion."]

407. see. [Emendation of Kittredge for E. E. T. S. *be*]; "see here the devil in a band." [Apparently a proverbial allusion — one unfamiliar to the present annotator. It is possible that *band* may mean " rope," and this may be another reference to the likelihood of Mak's getting hanged; there may have been a current saying in regard to the devil in a

rope or shackle, though in this case one would expect the plural. Or it is barely possible that *band* has its sense equivalent to our *bond*, " covenant, agreement." From some such current saying as " There 's the devil in the bond," i. e. " There 's trouble in this arrangement," such a phrase might arise, meaning " the devil to pay."]

409. note: sound.

411, 412. I may not sit at my work a " hand-long " while [i. e. time to walk a hand's breadth — time was currently expressed in terms of space to be walked, the rate being about three miles an hour].

414. Naught . . . takes: And does naught but take her pleasure.

416. D' ye suppose.

421. That lacks a woman.

429. great bellow: foul noise.

431. Yea . . . ill: I assent me thereto.

431. use . . . sleight: do as thou didst promise.

432. with skill *added*.

451. say it not *added*.

455. Horbury Shrogs. [I. e. Horbury thickets — *shrogs* denoting rough land covered with such thickets. Harbury is a town near Wakefield, with which the Towneley cycle is identified. The thorn tree of l. 403 is another local allusion, apparently, as there was a famous thorn tree called the " Shepherd's Thorn" in the neighborhood: see England and Pollard, E. E. T. S., *Introduction.*]

457. ewe. [The gender of the sheep changes later.]

467. quick sped: I counsel.

468. till . . . complete: the truth till I know.

470. bed: rest.

477. break: " crack " [i. e. " sing loudly."]

478. wake there *added*.

485. in . . . throes: i. e. in distress.

486. than . . . woes: than that she should have any disease.

487. well sped *added*.

487. O . . . grows: I may not well " queasse " [meaning unknown].

489. woe 's me *added*.

494. a bit *added*.

496. can . . . it: remember ye one yet?

497. my . . . hit: my dream this is it.

504. Nay, neither amends our mood, drink or meat.

509. I swear *added*.

517. got: fetched.

527. that 's plain *added*.

528. amain *added*.

530. there 's the door *added*.

534. I die *added*.

541. though *added*.

543. and such matters *added*.

548. " cattle." [The old form is retained, as a pun is intended on the two senses of the word — now differentiated in our *cattle* and *chattel*.]

552. each, one *added*.

558. To his hips in good time and in happiness [i. e. " a fortunate future and happiness be to him in body," *hips* typifying the whole body. The phrase is a forced one to provide a rime for *gossips*, but its artificiality would not have seemed so great to a mediæval hearer, owing to the practice of constantly referring to various parts of the body in blessing and cursing (cf. *lips*, l. 560, again to provide a rime). Moreover, reference to the hip in a generic sense was frequent in the phrase " on the hip," " on his hip," " on my hips," to denote a bad plight].

560. trust me *added*.

562, 563. [Gibbon Waller and John Horne are two of the shepherds in the *First Shepherds' Play* of the same cycle. The author borrowed these, but not the name of the third, there called by his first name or nickname Slowpace.]

564. fun and play: " garray " [i. e. " hubbub, excitement," here presumably " sport, hilarity "].

574. here: there.

577. little . . . mild: that little day-star.

591, 592. See note on *Everyman*, l. 316.

596. "A fals skawde hang at the last." [Manly reads this "A! false skawde, hang at the last," i. e. "Ah, thou false scold, hang at the last." It seems preferable to regard it as a proverb, emending *hang* to *hangys*, "A false scold hangs at the last," leading naturally to the next line, "So shalt thou!"]

613. mis-spoken. [Mak tries to make out that the supposed child has been put under a spell. Gill goes him one better by trying to make out that an elf has substituted a changeling for the true child, as the elves were supposed to do with children in order to have them for servants.]

614. This is a false work.

615. go *added*.

619. so *added*.

620. Ye two are surely at one [literally "bound together"] in one place [i. e. in this matter].

621. let . . . dead: let us do them to death. [The attribution of this speech, which is given to the third shepherd by E. E. T. S., is corrected by Manly.]

623. At . . . remain: with you will I be left; instead *added*.

625. in spite *added*.

629. in back and breast *added*.

632. therefore *added*.

638. attend ye *added*.

642. He commands.

646. Betwixt two beasts [the ox and the ass of tradition]

656. how . . . hear: heard ye not how he cracked it.

657. Marry . . . ear: Yea, marry he sang it clear and loud [introduced in next line].

667. not of woe *added*.

673. We have it not to lose.

675. therein *added*.

676. clergy. [Clerkly learning, inspiration.]

681. Ecce: *Cité* [E. E. T. S., corrected by Kölbing; the quotation is from *Isaiah* vii, 14].

691. gracious: "mener" [meaning not known].

692. beforne. [Used till the seventeenth century, and dialectically and archaically still later.]

702. First find and declare by his messenger.

704. to be there *added ;* with cheer *added.*

717. I have held my promise.

718. [The gifts given vary in the several Shepherds' Plays. In the Chester Play, the shepherds give a bell, a flask and spoon, and a cap, Garcius gives a pair of his wife's old hose (for other jewels he has none except his good heart and his prayers), and the "Boys" give a bottle, a hood, a shepherd's pipe, and a nut-hook. In the York Play, the shepherds give a brooch with a tin bell, two cob-nuts on a band, and a horn spoon. In the First Shepherds' Play of the Towneley cycle, the gifts are a "little spruce coffer," a ball, and a bottle.

723. from far *added.*

724. mop. [Literally, "fool," used like *moppet,* "silly," *rogue,* as a term of endearment.]

728. indeed *added.*

737. this night *added.*

738. aright: in seven.

752. safe and sound *added ;* Come forth transferred to l. 753.

EVERYMAN

45. in briefest space: in all haste.

48. passions to be: tempests.

50. and tarry not *added.*

75. dread: abhor.

88. For what *added.*

107. true *added.*

120. yet *added.*

125. or such gear *added.*

126. **prince, or peer** : duke nor prince.

148. **Saint Charity.** [" Holy Charity "; cf. Saint Cross, Saint Sepulchre.]

190. **would be** : had been.

191. **God wot** *added.*

206. **by this day** ! [One of many curious mediæval expletives. Fellowship uses it again in l. 236.]

221. **gramercy.** [Fr. *grant merci*, literally "great thanks, thanks exceedingly."]

284. **Fellowship** : Fellow[ship].

298. **I pray God take thee** : to God I commend thee.

301. **ending** : end [read *ending* riming with *grieving*].

316. [A proverb used to assert the force of " nature," which enables it to produce effects from causes, even in cases where obstacles, apparently insuperable, are in the way. The meaning here is that blood-relationship will force Everyman's kin to aid him in his distress even though they shrink and wish to refuse him.]

320. **Cousin.** [Then, as often still to-day, used as a general, as well as specific, title of relationship.]

324. **we.** [Omitted in original.]

348. **Alas, that ever I was born** !

359. **coax and court** : entice.

361. **to . . . sport** : to be foolish.

362. **in antics to take part** : " abroad to start " [i. e. " to break loose from ordinary restrictions, ' have a time,' ' carry on.' "]

363. **willingly** *added.*

373. **lo** *added.*

380. **and . . . refrain** : and nothing will do, indeed.

385. **for . . . provide** : to provide myself with.

392. [Goods, as later similarly Good Deeds, was presumably disclosed in a special booth by the raising of a curtain or similar device, as in Mr. Ben Greet's performances, in which Goods occupies a booth on one side of the stage, Good Deeds on the other, with the raised platform for the tomb or grave between them at the back.]

CPSIA information can be obtained at www.ICGtesting.com
Printed in the USA
LVOW101516110612

285603LV00009B/115/P

Riverside College Classics

THE
SECOND SHEPHERDS' PLAY
EVERYMAN

AND OTHER EARLY PLAYS

*TRANSLATED WITH INTRODUCTION
AND NOTES*

BY

CLARENCE GRIFFIN CHILD

PROFESSOR OF ENGLISH IN THE
UNIVERSITY OF PENNSYLVANIA

HOUGHTON MIFFLIN COMPANY
BOSTON   NEW YORK   CHICAGO   SAN FRANCISCO
The Riverside Press Cambridge

The Riverside Press
CAMBRIDGE . MASSACHUSETTS
PRINTED IN THE U . S . A